Due

The Faith of Jesus

The Faith of Jesus

A Study for Inquiring Christians

by IRA JAY MARTIN, 3rd

AN EXPOSITION–UNIVERSITY BOOK

EXPOSITION PRESS • NEW YORK

Biblical quotations in this book are taken from the *Revised Standard Version of the Bible,* copyrighted 1946 and 1952 by the Division of Christian Education, National Council of Churches, and are used by permission.

EXPOSITION PRESS INC., 386 Fourth Avenue, New York 16, N.Y.

FIRST EDITION

© 1956 by Ira Jay Martin, 3rd. *All rights reserved, including the right of reproduction in whole or in part in any form.* Manufactured in the United States of America. Library of Congress catalog card number: 56-8718.

ACKNOWLEDGMENTS

The words on the following pages are out of my mind and heart, but that I owe much to many lecturers and writers is apparent. I am deeply indebted to Dr. Robert H. Pfeiffer, of the Harvard Divinity School, for his continuous friendship and constant encouragement of my writing efforts through the years. I also owe a debt of gratitude to the Rev. Bruce Roberts, of the Syracuse Council of Churches, for his encouragement in the final stages of manuscript preparation.

I wish to express my thanks for the critical readings of Dr. W. Gordon Ross, head of my department at Berea College, Kentucky, who guided me into sharper expression and helped revise many impressions, and of Mrs. Jo Richards Haywood of New Orleans, former student secretary and my English critic. Other student secretaries have assisted in typing various chapters through the years; to them I extend my gratitude. Finally, I wish to thank the Division of Christian Education of the National Council of Churches of Christ in the United States of America for their kind permission to quote from the American Standard Version and the Revised Standard Version.

The final work, of course, is mine, with all its shortcomings in insight or literary expression.

IRA JAY MARTIN, 3RD

CONTENTS

I	INTRODUCTION	11
	The Meaning of "Faith"	12
	The Status of Jesus	13
II	THE FAITH THAT INFLUENCED HIM	15
	Normative Judaism	15
	Hellenistic Judaism	20
	Joseph—Mary	23
III	THE FAITH HE EXPERIENCED	29
	At the Age of Twelve	29
	His Baptism	31
	His Temptation Experience	32
	A Crisis	36
	Another Crisis—Near Caesarea Philippi	39
	The Transfiguration	44
	The Resurrection in the Faith of Jesus	47
	A Further Crisis	48
	On the Cross	50
IV	THE FAITH HE LIVED	53
	In Regard to His Own Family	53
	In Regard to His Rivals	55
	In Regard to His Contemporaries	57
	In Regard to His Enemies	64
	In Regard to Himself	66
	In Regard to His Participation in the Religious Practices of His Day	71
	Summary	74
V	THE FAITH HE EXPECTED	75

VI	THE FAITH HE SHARED	92
	From Q	93
	From L	108
	From M	123
	From "Mark"	137
VII	THE FAITH THAT WAS IN HIM	144
	God	146
	The World	150
	Man	153
	Sin	154
	The Means of Salvation	156
	Salvation	159
	The Kingdom of God	163
	Himself	167
VIII	THE FAITH THAT MOTIVATED HIM	173
	Principle 1: In the Beginning God	175

(a) God is a Person, 175. (b) God as King, Legislator and Judge, 176. (c) God knows all, and knows best, 177. (d) Man can depend upon God's Providence, 177.

Principle 2: God Created the Earth ... 178
(a) The earth is good, beautiful and friendly, 178. (b) Man should respect the earth, 179. (c) All property is a stewardship, 179.

Principle 3: Man Made in God's Image ... 180
(a) Man is crown and summit of God's creativity, 180. (b) Each individual is a son of God, 180. (c) Respect for personality, 180.

Principle 4: Man in Need of Maturation ... 183
(a) Man's basic incompleteness, 184. (b) Release of man's potentialities, 185. (c) Human betterment, 185.

Principle 5: Faith Is the Key ... 186
(a) Conduct is the by-product of character, 186. (b) Seek ye first the Kingdom, 187.

Principle 6: The Ultimate for Man Is a Natural Goodness ... 188

Principle 7: A Relationship of Love ... 190
(a) Love is the law of life, 191. (b) Grace, undeserved mercy, 191. (c) The forgiving God, 191. (d) As God treats men, so man will treat his fellow man, 192. (e) Superior righteousness, 192.

Principle 8: A New Society ... 193
(a) The Kingdom of God, 194. (b) The Kingdom is God's, 195. (c) It is a Kingdom, 195. (d) The citizens of the Kingdom are not slaves, 195.

Principle 9: Death Is a Fact ... 196
(a) Physical death is a fact, 197. (b) Jesus was concerned with "inward" death, 197.

Principle 10: Being Is Immortal ... 198
(a) The soul is immortal, 199. (b) Jesus expected his own death and resurrection, 200. (c) Eternal identity, 201.

A Concluding Remark ... 202

EPILOGUE ... 205

CHAPTER I

INTRODUCTION

Each generation discovers its dire need for a vital faith with which to confront its problems and to cast out its fears. Especially is this true today. Modern scientific advancement is persistently outdistancing the moral restraints of men; modern psychology is challenging the power and validity of all external controls. Chaos exists in all its potential fury just below the surface of man's life—personal and communal. Unless each generation takes positive action to develop the inner disciplines it may very well destroy itself. Almost instinctively, one comes to realize how vital this factor of self-control is in building a desirable life, home, community, nation and world. Such inner motivations and restraints are the by-products of the individual's philosophy of life—of his religious faith. To be of value, this faith must be a *living faith*, fervent and vigorous. It must be a faith to give the individual confidence in his quest for self-control.

His search inevitably leads him to the great extant religions. He notes that all of them, with the exception of Hinduism, come from the historic period 650 B.C. to A.D. 650. Moreover, all except Hinduism have been established around an heroic personality. The various faiths have developed around the founder and his teachings: the founder to whom men give their allegiance; his teachings which discipline the minds and motivate the actions of his followers. Ultimately the seeker is attracted to the young Nazarene and his faith, traditionally called Christianity.

Despite the fact that the historic Christian church has also patterned its faith around its Founder, the time is long overdue for a fresh study of his life and thought in order to discover anew those aspects of the faith which may guide and stimulate young Christians into a vital and vigorous faith of their own. Traditionally we have been more concerned with the faith in and about Jesus. The purpose of this study is to discover and portray the faith of Jesus himself, in order to ascertain the secrets of his artistry and the techniques by which he built a refreshing vibrant life.

The faith of Jesus! Did Jesus have faith? Did Jesus live by faith? This entails two vital questions of primary importance: What is meant by faith? And what is the status of Jesus contained in this study?

The Meaning of "Faith"

Faith! What is faith? What is involved in faith? Already we have been using the word with two distinct meanings. "Faith" has been used first as a term designating a distinct set of doctrines, rituals and devotional practices that constitute that which we speak of as the Hindu faith or the Christian faith. Then we used the word to refer to that sense and act of trust and assurance which comes as the result of an accumulation of responses to knowledge, testing and self-surrender thereto. It is with this latter aspect of Jesus' faith that we will be most concerned. The proper relationship of these two aspects of the word "faith" is of grave significance. The meaningful doctrinal faith for any individual should be a conscious outgrowth in terms of cultic practice and intellectual interpretation of actual experiences of faith. For usually one lives according to one's faith rather than one's doctrines. Therefore, when we speak of "the faith of Jesus" we are most concerned with those trusts and assurances we see developing from his multiple opportunities for testing and trusting those areas of knowledge which came to him through experience, as well as through heritage, observation and insight. We are determined to discover those fundamental truths, principles and attitudes by which Jesus lived and died,

Introduction 13

and through which, we are persuaded, present-day Christians will find more abundant living.

The Status of Jesus

Did Jesus have faith? Did Jesus live by faith? These questions are a little more difficult to answer than is at first suspected. If one says that Jesus was deity, then the question is raised: Why did he need faith? If one says that Jesus was human, orthodoxy is challenged. The common, orthodox Christian's idea of Jesus is something on this order: Jesus came into this world not by human processes but by an act of will on God's part. He was born of a virgin, and from the very day of his birth the divine mind and soul were in him—wise men as well as shepherds worshipped him as king. He was aware of his messianic dignity from the very first. He received his messianic consecration in the Jordan River at the hands of a prepared forerunner, John the Baptist. He then retired to the wilderness to settle with a personal devil the issues of his messiahship. He thereupon entered a public ministry which brought crowds streaming to his person. The common people accepted him as Messiah; the aristocrats rejected him. And as the Messiah, Jesus was condemned, as prophesied in Isaiah 53:1–12, and died on the cross, all according to the foreordained will of God.

"What is the matter with those ideas?" asks the sincere fundamentalist Christian. "The Scriptures, especially the four Gospels, give that picture of the Man of Nazareth, and who are we to question the holy Word of God as presented in the sacred Scriptures?" We must agree with this person, because the four Gospels taken as a unit give that impression of Jesus. Yet, after devout and careful research, when all the coatings of tradition, dogma and theology have been removed, a most refreshing and vivid portrait of the Nazarene comes forth. The original is more wonderful than the retouchings that have tried to enhance it. The Jesus we discover is a being who is truly alive to God as well as to man. He is a soul whom the circumstances of a simple, pious Jewish family, among the class of the *am-ha-aretz*, have tempered into a God-guided, God-conscious, God-like person. We find a being who, from birth to death, lived by a "childlike" faith and simple trust in God and His universe. We see an infant soul grow "in the good soil" from a self-centered youngster into a God-centered man. We watch him buffet his way through the last three (?) years of his life against all temptations, choosing the higher values of life because back in those hidden years he had learned from experience that God rewards all those who are faithful and obedient to His Will. When we try to recapture those days of actual earthly experience of Jesus we lose all sense of self-conscious messiahship on his part. In its place, we find him conscious of a new life which he sought to share, a life that was lived by "childlike" faith and by complete obedience to God's Will. This is the true Gospel, the Good News which he proclaimed and which he sought to share.

Let us, therefore, with realistic endeavor enter into the presence of the Master of Life with a devout desire to learn of him and of his faith that casteth out all fear.

CHAPTER II

THE FAITH THAT INFLUENCED HIM

Every man coming into the world is beset by a system of ideas that seeks to enslave his mind and to dull his perceptions and insights against eventual escape from it. This was no less true for Jesus of Nazareth. Even before his own consciousness was aware of its identity, the fundamental faith of his neighbors and family was encompassing him by its ethical responses, intellectual expositions, and its ritualistic practices carried on unconsciously in everyday living, gossip and discussion. The basic demands of the Jewish faith were given lip-service, at least, by the local rabbi, by the devout Pharisees (the argumentative minds of the town) and in parental discussions and paternal pronouncements within the family circle. Thus we are compelled by the course of events in every man's life to enunciate the religious faith and practices of the environment into which the Babe of Bethlehem was thrust.

Normative Judaism

The Exile in Babylon had done something for and to the Hebrew religion. Enforced separation from Israelite territory had caused the Hebrew people to cherish that which had gone almost unnoticed up to that time: the true significance and value of the religious literature of the past. Its sacredness became immediately apparent to the devout prophet and priest; and the office of scribe arose to take care of ferreting out religious manuscripts brought by the exiles to Babylon. Once catalogued, the more significant rolls were copied; some were integrated;

and all were "corrected" under priestly surveillance. The remainder, if any, were left uncopied and have been for the most part lost to posterity. This intensive research resulted in a new expression of Hebrew religion, which we have come to know as Judaism.

The preservation and study of these manuscripts resulted in two other innovations in the religious life of the people: the synagogue (which is primarily a school) and the rabbi (whose chief function is to instruct). As the scribes did their scholarly work, the rabbis transmitted the basic ideas into popular concepts whereby the new generation might comprehend the sacred truths revealed to the forefathers. The result was the unconscious exaltation of the Torah, and the unwitting replacing of experiential faith by a doctrinal faith evolved from the systematic study of the Torah. Not only did Ezekiel prescribe a renovated ritual for a restored Temple in Jerusalem, but unnamed ritualists began the stabilization of all the religious activities of the individual. A system of home rituals was brought into being, which in one way helped to solidify these frustrated exiles into a common fellowship; but in another way it enslaved the spiritually awakening and developing Jewish youth in a strait jacket of creed, ceremony and uncreative religiosity. Of this Jesus became very much aware during his unrecorded adolescence. His adult ministry reveals his strenuous efforts to retrieve the creative spirit of prophetic religion.

Into the first-century expression of normative Judaism Jesus was born. In order to envision the whole picture of Jesus' faith and practice, therefore, we should examine the predominant doctrines and practices of normative Judaism, many of which Jesus unquestioningly assumed in his teaching ministry.

For the Jew of Jesus' day, religion was something revealed. God was conceived as having made His Will partially known to earlier spiritual leaders of mankind like Adam and Noah. Further and more detailed revelations were given to their Hebrew forebears, the patriarchs Abraham, Isaac and Jacob; yet reserved for Moses was the full and complete revelation of God's truth and wisdom. This revealed Word of God was thought to be contained in the Torah, which was accredited to Moses. The later prophets of the eighth and seventh centuries were regarded merely as interpreters of this Torah. By the first century, a sizable amount of so-called "oral tradition" had been added to these written "commentaries" on the Torah, and the combined aggregate of "written" and "oral" tradition served to guide the Pharisees of Jesus' day in establishing a system of proper conduct for the Jewish community. The scribes thought religion consisted in perfect knowledge of the Torah and perfect observance of it to the minutest prescription. Normative Judaism, therefore, must be regarded chiefly as a way of life rather than as a system of thought—a way of life evolved out of the refining experiences of a people consciously seeking to do the Will of God.

Equally important with the Jewish concept of revealed religion is the belief in ethical monotheism. From time immemorial, the Jew had believed in the Oneness of God. The Shema is the evidence for this dogma in normative Judaism. God is One; and this One God was portrayed as all-powerful, all-knowing, all-righteous and ever-present. The destiny of human history was in His Hands. Nothing was thought to be able to thwart Him in His purpose or in the execution of His Will. He had loved and covenanted with the Jewish forefathers; now He was ready to love all those who would sensitize their obedient souls to His Will and Wisdom. His chief concern in regard to man was His desire that man might truly fulfill His purposes in reflecting His moral character. Normative Judaism was no mere philosophical monotheism; it was an *ethical* monotheism established upon the unity of the moral order in the history of the world. Belief in One God implied a single world religion to first-century Jewry.

Sin was therefore conceived chiefly as any lack of moral conformity to the prescriptions of the Torah, as interpreted by the "written" or "oral" traditions of the faith. This nonconformity may be the result of willful disobedience, or of ignorant action. Thus the pharisaic concern for exactitude was at the point of proper conduct. In a sense, sin was primarily a social responsibility; i.e., the people were collectively responsible for some individual sins as well as for community sin. Individuals, however, could not escape a certain amount of condemnation. In order to right these wrongs, expiations and purifications were prescribed to carry out what were believed to be the conditions of God's forgiveness; and the individual's moral transgression was corrected through repentance and the scapegoat ritual on the Day of Atonement. Injuries to one's neighbor's person, property or good name could be resolved only through genuine confession, prayer for forgiveness, earnest desire and endeavor to avoid falling into the sin again, and by becoming increasingly obedient to the Will of God as revealed in the Torah.

Salvation was conceived as life lived according to the Will of God revealed in the Torah. Yet no Jew hoped to achieve such perfection in this life, no matter how hard he tried. The day would come when God's Will would be obeyed implicitly. Judgment would fall upon all who had failed morally and religiously to reform their lives through genuine repentance. A part of this concept was what became known as "the messianic hope." Born sometime during the Babylonian Exile, the messianic hope sustained the Jew in his desire for freedom of body, mind and soul. This Golden Age was portrayed in idyllic imagery inspired by the idealizing of the two past monarchial periods of political freedom: Davidic and Maccabean. The Jew dreamed of the day when he would be free from foreign domination to live his own life, to follow his own religious leanings unhindered and to enjoy the favor of God. Some of the Jews desired a restored monarchy; others preferred no earthly sovereign, but God Himself. Thus the Jew thought in terms of a theocracy rather than a hierarchy.

Concerning immortality, the Judean Jew was slightly more conservative than his Hellenistic fellow men. He believed that at the end of this present age there was to be a universal judgment. Until that moment, the dead resided in Sheol, a place of shades. At the time of judgment, the "dead" would be resurrected (i.e., resuscitated) *in toto* (i.e., body, mind and spirit), and the resurrected whole person would then stand before the throne of the

Divine Judge and be judged. The twofold indictments were these: the just would live forever on a transfigured earth, exempt from all infirmities of the flesh and evils of the present world, and the wicked were doomed to an unquenchable fire. Such ideas were rejected by the Sadducees because they found no basis for them in the Torah. The Pharisees, however, were more zealous in the belief.

The suffering of the righteous had once been thought to reveal the sins of their souls, but by Jesus' day the affliction of such people was regarded as evidence of discipline. It would appear that such suffering was no longer thought of as punishment but as "a refining fire." The prosperity of the wicked, on the other hand, was considered God's way of allowing them to heap sin upon sin, so to speak, unto their utter condemnation. (Prosperity, it must be remembered, had once been thought to give evidence of Divine favor.)

The true character of normative Judaism can be thoroughly grasped only through a detailed study of its entire nature: authentic teachings, cultic practices and ethical by-products in the lives of its devotees. Only a few of its more distinctive features have been summarized above. Yet it must be said in all fairness to the Palestinian scene of the first century that the religion of the plain man (of the *am-ha-aretz*) was rather shallow in contrast to this profound subsoil of the faith. Religion for the peasant was the carrying out of conventional requirements: observing the major feasts and fasts, keeping the Sabbath and holy days, paying the prescribed tithes and offerings, attending the synagogue and making pilgrimages to the Temple in Jerusalem. This entailed learning and practicing innumerable cultic activities in home, synagogue and Temple, many of which had lost their connections with ethical living. Despite this emphasis upon the ceremonial, the Jew was concerned chiefly with the conduct of men. Yet perhaps the ministry and message of John the Baptist shows the prevalent lack of balance in the religion of Jesus' day. The Nazarene's own ministry likewise indicates the contemporary unfortunate concern for the ritual and the ceremony.

Such was the form of Judaism which was advocated and taught by the local rabbis and about which the youthful Jesus argued with the doctors in the Temple. We may assume that this statement of normative Judaism was simply the ideal toward which the Jew struggled in belief and action. The actual living faith was something else again, as in every generation. Yet this was the faith they were willing not only to struggle to live by but to die for.

Hellenistic Judaism

The conquests of Alexander the Great (332–321 B.C.) spread the liberating spirit of Hellenism throughout the ascetic, rigorous Near East. During the first century B.C. and the early part of the first century of the Christian era, the Jews of Palestine not only were encircled by Hellenism but were responding to its challenge both with rebuff, as under the Maccabees, and Judean orthodoxy and with compromising willingness, as in the Diaspora and to some degree in Galilee. Traversed by major caravan routes, more accessible than mountainous Judea, Galilee found itself becoming quite cosmopolitan and slightly more liberal under the Hellenizing influence of culturally aggressive Syria to the north.

What was this Hellenizing influence? How did it affect the nature of Judaism in thought and action as lived and expressed in Galilee? Hellenism, in a sense the civilizing power in Galilean society, invaded every aspect of life. The liberal ideas of Hellenic culture affected the organization, legislation and administration of the local government, and they created an interest in the arts and what we might call the sciences. The customs and costumes of Galilee were also influenced by this new spirit.

When Hellenism came into contact with Judaism, tensions came into being. The Greeks loved life to the full, while the Jew, because of his nomadic heritage, was content with a more ascetic way of life. This difference in emphasis was most marked by the individual's thought regarding his body. The Greek treated the body as the beautiful house of the eternal soul, to be swept and garnished, so to speak. The Hebrew, on the other hand, regarded it simply as the outer material garment of the total being, controlled by an "inner man." Hellenic games gave expression to Greek pride in the flesh and respect for the temple of the indestructible soul. Jewish nomadic asceticism, and a sort of native modesty which kept the body forever covered to the eyes of man, were expressive of the Jew's almost distasteful disregard for the flesh. This was undoubtedly due in part to the dusty and rigorous existence in the almost waterless wastes of the Near East. Perhaps the Hellenic ideal, seeping into the thought-world of Galilee, came to serve as one of the causes for Jesus' high regard for physical health and happiness, leading him into a healing ministry.

The Greek thought in abstractions. He was given to philosophizing about life; he was tinged with mysticism. The Jew, on the other hand, was very much a "realist," or should we say a "literalist"? He could not think of love or faith apart from actual incidents of love and faith. The Kingdom of God was conceived in very realistic earthly terms; "disembodied" love, faith and the Kingdom of God were just not a part of ordinary Jewish thinking and expectations. Yet Jesus seems to have bridged the gap, for he takes the phrase "the Kingdom of God" and transforms it from an earthly monarchy to a spiritual realm wherein God is King of men's souls. He takes earthly love and refines it into a Divine Love so amazing that it includes the outcast and the enemy. He takes the simple experience of trust and makes it the Way of Salvation: "thy faith has made thee whole."

Greek ability to be economically prosperous can also be noted in Galilee. Partly because of extensive trade routes running through that area, and partly because of financially wise Gentiles, prosperity flourished in the cities that clustered about the Sea of Galilee. The Decapolis area, with its definite Hellenic culture, helped the area generally to be economically better off. Isolated Judea was more poverty-stricken and depended in large measure upon the tithes and offerings brought to the Holy City. The following listing may indicate the intellectual and spiritual conflicts in the midst of which Jesus was reared in Galilee:

<ul style="list-style:none">
<li>Greek polytheism   vs. Hebrew monotheism</li>
<li>Greek freedom   vs. Hebrew restraint</li>
<li>Greek wealth   vs. Hebrew poverty</li>
<li>Greek complexity   vs. Hebrew simplicity</li>
<li>Greek radicalism   vs. Hebrew conservatism</li>
<li>Greek philosophy   vs. Hebrew religion</li>
<li>Greek love of the physical vs. Hebrew love of the spiritual</li>
</ul>

To indicate the Hellenistic religious spirit in the area, we only need mention three cities near Nazareth. Eighteen miles to the east of Jesus' boyhood home lay Scythopolis (old Bethshean), where in Jesus' day the cult of Bacchus held full sway. It was, in fact, the chief city in the Decapolis district and was said to surpass even Jerusalem in both population and splendor. The hill on which the city lay was crowned by a beautiful temple to Dionysus (or Bacchus). At about half the distance to Scythopolis was the newly constructed Graeco-Roman city of Tiberias, named after the reigning Caesar. Nestled on the shores of the renamed Sea of Galilee (Lake Tiberius), the new city was the stronghold and propaganda center for Hellenism. The rumor is that Jews were forbidden to have anything to do with it because Tiberias reportedly was built on top of a Jewish cemetery; whether Jesus as a carpenter had anything to do directly or indirectly with its construction makes interesting speculation. Then, just across the valley to the north of Nazareth, was Sepphoris. In the valley was one of the richest caravan routes wending its way from the East to the Mediterranean. Sepphoris had been totally destroyed by the Romans, and in Jesus' day was rebuilt by Herod Antipas. This city, too, was a stronghold of Hellenistic culture, broadcasting its civilizing spirit and its pagan religious thought to the surrounding area. Whether or not Jesus had any part in its rebuilding is likewise not known.

The nearness of these centers of Hellenistic culture undoubtedly filled the social and intellectual as well as the religious and spiritual atmosphere of Jesus' home with a liberalizing, though paganizing, spirit. This may have influenced Jesus' attitudes toward the Sabbath, the washing of hands before eating, the Samaritans, children, women, those called "dogs" (foreigners) and his other points of contention with the more conservative and orthodox convictions of the relatively isolated Judeans.

In Hellenistically influenced Galilee Jesus grew up. He appears to have been challenged by these alien ideas and ideals, responding to them no matter how conservative and reactionary adults sought to warn and to rescue him from such "paganism." We probably cannot explain the genius of Jesus by Hellenism in any form, yet that he went free from its influence is most unlikely. His struggle with the Judean hierarchy is probably the clearest evidence of his Hellenically tinted spirit of liberty, humanitarianism and filial piety to God. This undoubtedly was one of the many influences that caused Jesus and his disciples to be at variance with the more conservative element in Judaism centered about Jerusalem.

Joseph—Mary

Any statement in regard to Jesus' religious home life by necessity must be highly speculative. Yet we are persuaded that some statement should be made. These comments will be reconstructed upon the basis of scriptural evidence whenever possible. We are very much aware that the accounts upon which we rely have been greatly influenced by the interests and aims of the earliest storytellers. This fact may mislead us in our restoration of the situation, yet we are persuaded that behind the records are solid traditions and elements of historic fact.

Despite one's own high respect for the Christology regarding the Man of Nazareth, one wonders what his life would have been if his home experience had been adverse. Suppose, for instance, what Jesus' life would have been if he had had a shiftless and irresponsible mother?—a drunkard or an immoral woman for a mother? One may feel that these are unnecessary interrogations, yet the point we seek to make is that Mary's own devout and religious spirit must have been one of the molding influences on Jesus' life. Her own spontaneous enthusiastic participation in the little home rituals of religion probably sensitized the youthful Jesus to things spiritual. Although no textual references are available, we can rest assured from the other evidence revealed in Jesus' life and teachings that Mary and Joseph maintained with pious devotion, perhaps beyond the ordinary family in Nazareth, home expressions of religious faith and practice.

In addition to the multitudinous cares and practices of a young mother with her children, especially the recently born, Mary—or some other hard-working woman close to Jesus (certainly not Joseph, the busy carpenter)—helped to develop the love and appreciation of nature that Jesus later exhibited. From such an interest Jesus received many of his poignant illustrations and parables. His awareness of God's watch-care over the lilies, the birds and the foxes helped develop his concepts of and faith in Divine Providence over mankind. As the oldest child, Jesus may very well have developed his unusual love for children and women from the early training of Mary by caring for the younger children and easing of her load. "Suffer the little children to come unto me" may be only a later manifestation of this early experience and training in the respect for human personality that was one of the foci of his faith, practice and teaching. Value of persons as well as things may have been the influence of Mary's faith upon his. One wonders if the unnamed woman who cleaned her home in search for a lost coin (Luke 15:8–10) could have been Mary. It was undoubtedly Mary's tender care and loving concern not only for her son and husband but for the neighbors that helped develop the compassion which Jesus had for his fellow men.

There are three distinctly recorded occasions of the mother-and-child relationship which may serve as windows into her faith. Mary's tender remarks as reported in the Lucan account of the Temple visit of the youthful Jesus (Luke 2:41–52) show the sterling quality of her personality. No harsh words, no nagging unreasonable language, nothing but winsome concern. Now that Jesus "was a man," her days of training were over; the period for guidance was at hand. Wise insights were these for a humble, untutored young country matron. Such quality of character undoubtedly greatly enriched Jesus' growing personality. The account of Mary's quest for the "misguided teacher" (John 10:20, Mark 3:21; cf. Mark 3:31–35, Matthew 12:49–50, Luke 8:19–21) reveals a different Mary from that whom we usually conjure up in our minds. Here she is portrayed as incapable of comprehending her oldest son's recent actions and teachings. The same concern is present, but she has allowed the situation to compel her to take drastic action, and encouraged and assisted by her four other sons, she makes her fruitless attempt to take him home. Jesus' rebuff of Mary apparently enlightened her concerning his motives, or at least caused her to rationalize the facts, because we next encounter her at the foot of the cross. Whether or not the fourth Gospel (John 10:25–27) faithfully records the situation is a question; by taking the text at its face value as based upon historical facts, we see a remorseful mother whose faith has been restored in this unusual son. Unlike her next-oldest son James, Jesus had not chosen the way of pharisaic obedience to the Torah; rather, he had evolved a more spiritual way of life through intimate communion with God as Father. In this, Jesus had followed Mary in her spiritual life. Thus we see a lovable, simple but sensitive and alert Galilean matron unwittingly imparting her faith to her son, whose vigorous mind, soul and will extended that faith into a universally redeeming reality.

Of Joseph, not much is known. For instance, our inquisitive minds would like the answers to these questions: How old was he in comparison with Mary? How old was he when Jesus was born? How old was Jesus when Joseph died? Was Joseph really Jesus' father after all?

What we know is that Joseph was a carpenter by trade, and in accordance with Jewish custom would attempt to teach his son the trade. If the birth stories reveal any historic facts, and we believe they do, one is that Joseph was gifted with a generous amount of sympathy. His concern for Mary's condition on the trip to Bethlehem reveals this tenderness of soul; his respect for Mary, in contrast to the paternalistic customs of the usual Jewish father, is revealed in his being merely a silent bystander in the reunion of mother and child in the Temple of Jerusalem when Jesus was twelve years of age (cf. Luke 2:41–52). There appears on the latter occasion no show of anger, disgust or restlessness because of loss of the time consumed in returning and ferreting out the lost son. Everything appears to be taken in stride —the mark of a well-balanced personality.

Furthermore, one is tempted to see behind the illustrations of the easy yoke (Matthew 11:29–30), the houses built on sand and rock (Matthew 7:24–27) and the man who tore down his barns in expectation of building bigger ones (Luke 12:16–18) personal experiences of Joseph and Jesus working together, or, if Joseph has died too early for that to have happened, the results of Joseph's expert teaching Jesus the carpenter's trade. Such exactness and concern for the life involved, be it animal, man or a man's family, reveals a sensitive humanitarianism in Joseph which stimulated like responses in the life of his son.

The great imponderable in connection with Joseph, however, is the relation of Mary's husband to her son's concept of God as Father. Acknowledging the fact that God was already designated the Father of Israel (cf. Isaiah 63:16), scholars still accept the fact that Jesus individualized that Fatherhood and brought to it a filial ideal that not many Jewish rabbis would or could have realized. Perhaps Joseph's wholesomeness of character helped Jesus to formulate the attribute of God as Heavenly Father. To choose the descriptive term "Father" as his personal designation of God reveals something of Jesus' reverence for Joseph. The term would never have served his purpose if his own family experience had

The Faith That Influenced Him

not been almost ideal; a sullen or tyrannical Joseph would have prevented it. For an adult, unmarried Jesus, modern Freudianized psychology would almost demand a strong feminine influence before the Motherhood of God might be expected, despite the strong paternalistic mores of the Jewish people. Yet we see in Jesus' choice of the one word "Father," which to him signified his relationship to God, some influence and heroic adoration of Joseph. This may have been helped by the death of Joseph when the young boy needed his father most in the early adolescent years. Jesus must have idealized him very much! Perhaps in psychological response to Joseph's death, Jesus turned to his Heavenly Father for solace and beheld God in terms of Joseph. In defense of this possibility, one needs only to remember Isaiah's portrayal of God (chapter 6) in terms of the good King Uzziah, who had recently died.

One final comment can and should be made in regard to Joseph and Mary's religious influence upon Jesus. Their desire to make the long hazardous journey on foot from Nazareth to Jerusalem for Jesus' *bar mizvah* when it could have taken place in the local synagogue or assembly hall is evidence of Joseph and Mary's combined desire to give their children the best in religious experiences. Already, perhaps, they had come to recognize the seemingly unusual quality in the young boy, and no time or effort or expense was too great to enhance this momentous occasion in their son's life when he "became a man." One wonders if those fond parents did as much for the other four sons (Matthew 13:55). If the Acts' (15:13–21, cf. Gal. 2:12) portrayal of James (or Jacob) is anything like the actual person, we can see another type of response to the careful religious training which these Nazarene children got from their conscientious, devout parents.

These random ideas merely make us aware of the influence of Joseph and Mary upon the evolving life-faith of Jesus. How much was consciously taught by the parent, and how much was assimilated by the alert and sensitive mind and soul of Jesus, one can never know, but that such interaction was present and bore fruit which we can see in the recorded life of the adult Jesus is a certainty.

These are three of the four major points of influence in every man's life—the school-church, the community, and the home. From the manifestations of faith as taught, lived and shared in first-century Palestine, Jesus selected, rejected, adopted and adapted to fit his own experience, insight and divine revelation. The influence of this conglomerate faith is to be seen in the assumptions and practices of Jesus' devotional life and thought. Yet our attention is drawn to the fourth major point of influence in a man's life, the relation of his soul to God. This is the heart of all vital, renewing and redeeming faith. This is the key to Jesus' unique life, the core of his faith.

CHAPTER III

THE FAITH HE EXPERIENCED

The faith of the fathers has interest and concern only for the research scholar. One cannot really inherit faith; one may inherit only doctrinal statements. One may even intellectually accept these doctrines as adequate statements of religious belief, but the faith by which one lives day by day may be something completely different from the intellectual affirmations. It is with this personal element of faith as Jesus experienced it that we shall now concern ourselves.

It is generally recognized that the Gospel of Mark has given us the actual historic sequence of Jesus' life during his public ministry. We may assume, likewise, that Luke is trustworthy in recounting in his Gospel an earlier event in the life of Jesus, when at the age of twelve he participated in a significant Passover festival in Jerusalem. We may assume, however, that earlier experiences of a religious nature were a part of Jesus' growing personality. We have pointed out some of the areas in which devotional feelings and responses probably took place in Jesus' relationship to Joseph and Mary, and presumably to the neighbors' children, adult friends and the local rabbi. This chapter is concerned chiefly with those recorded experiences which greatly affected Jesus' personal growth. Some of these experiences he was led to share with his disciples and friends, and fortunately they helped to transmit them to posterity.

At the Age of Twelve
(Luke 2:41–52)

The episode of Jesus' visit with his parents to the Temple during Passover when he was twelve years old is of special interest in the study of the development of his faith. Although recorded only by Luke, it has strong probability as an historical event. The story reveals some of the early interests and inclinations of the boy who was to grow into God-like manhood. This episode in the Temple is of great importance, for it points up the faith of Jesus at a particular crisis in his adolescence: it reveals how deep-seated was the conception of God as Father in his thinking.

The twelfth year was an exciting time in the life of a Jewish boy. It was the period when his manhood was recognized and he became *bar mizvah,* a son of the covenant. Just when and where Jesus participated in this ritual of the faith is unknown; one may conjecture that it was in connection with the momentous visit to Jerusalem. We may assume, however, that the Lucan anecdote probably records his first official visit to the great Temple in the Holy City. The development of the youthful Jesus had proceeded according to the laws of human growth; the impressions and lessons of his childhood were fashioning his manhood. If the records contain no further elaboration of his pre-ministerial days, that is probably because he did not recount any and the early Christians therefore knew none. If he had told nothing of his childhood, there was nothing to tell, for "the stream ran quietly but deep." Yet out of childhood came the man, with faith in God as personal Father. In child fashion, he had taken to heart the contemporary concept of God as the Father of each Israelite—therefore his own Father, one to be trusted, one to be obeyed, one from whom to learn, and one with whom to live and have communion.

In this plain and simple account of a common and homely event in the life of the youthful Jesus, we see manifested the unfolding of a faith that was to become complete and supreme. It would appear that his whole life was beginning to be lived on a God-centered level rather than on a self-centered or even a parent-centered one. God's Will began to supersede his own will, even the will of his parents. His faith was that which he later expected of his disciples, a childlike faith. It was not so much intellectual (although it was not utterly unintellectual) as a simple trust in the ultimate and eternal personality, as of a son in a father. Through it, he believed, God expected him to reflect Him in human personality, to be truly in His image.

At His Baptism
(Mark 1:9–11; cf. Matthew 3:13–17, Luke 3:21–23)

The first authoritative account of Jesus comes with the narrative concerning his baptism. We should assume that the original story was told by Jesus himself, possibly during the sojourn near Tyre and Sidon, and it is probably he who chose the various symbols used in the story. This is the occasion in Jesus' manhood where our oldest extant narrative source, Mark, begins. Here we are presented with a full-grown man of some thirty years (Luke 3:23), full-blown in faith and spiritual quality as well as in physical growth and intellectual maturity. We as Christians have been content to think of Jesus as always an adult, in full possession of all of his faculties. We are prone to forget that before the flower come the seed, the stalk, the blade, but most of all the grooming, pruning and care that make the bloom perfect. The flower needs care, fertilizer, sun and rain, and a will to reflect the beauty of God.

> I asked the roses as they grew
> Richer and lovelier in their hue
> What made their tints so rich and bright.
> They answered, "Looking toward the light."
> Ah, secret, dear, sad heart of mine,
> God meant my life to be like thine,
> Radiant with heavenly beauty bright
> By simply looking toward the light.
> —Anon.

As Jesus learned this lesson from the lilies of the field, so he looked always toward the Light of God, the Father, and sought to have his life grow richer and lovelier in its hue. For it, his disciples have called him Messiah.

From the Gospel records, this moment on the bank of the Jordan River in the presence of John the Baptist appears to be the first vital decision Jesus made. His life had been tending toward it, as all of us know from similar experiences of our own. The supreme service which John rendered for mankind was to summon to consciousness the spiritual forces latent at this time in Jesus.

The whole experience is told in traditional imagery and symbolism well known to modern psychological explanations. Jesus' exalted consciousness of knowing and loving God caused him to hear God name him what he longed to be, a son of God. The sight of humanity eager for a meaningful, abundant life created in him the God-directed desire to share his experience of eternal-like life with all men, to help them discover God afresh to their souls, to call Israel (at least) to an absolute acceptance of the rule of God in human hearts. This is what he believed was the providence of God for all men: an eternal-like life centered in a complete faith in, and an abandoned obedience to, God as a personal Father. He felt that all men were called of God to be sons of God. He, for one, chose that goodly heritage for himself, and no one was to take it from him.

With the experience of baptism and the focusing of his various ideas and desires upon the Will of God as he saw it, he felt that he had entered the path God meant him to follow. He was profoundly conscious of his Father's approval of this act of decision and faith as the Will of God for him.

His Temptation Experience
(Matthew 4:1–11; cf. Luke 4:1–13)

The great decision of the baptismal hour was very significant. It is interesting to note that the earliest Gospel writer, who evidently had no recourse to the details of Jesus' temptation experience, relates the tradition, which probably stemmed from Jesus himself, how "the spirit drove him" into the wilderness to think things over.

Apparently unprepared for the requirements of such a momentous decision, Jesus, as was his custom, went apart to meditate and pray. Whether we are to assign the belief in a personal Satan to Jesus or to members of the early church is still a moot question. Even if Jesus personally did not believe in Satan as a person, he might have felt called upon to speak in terms familiar to his hearers. Whatever the explanation for the appearance of Satan in the story, the tradition leaves a strong impression of a personal struggle on the part of Jesus. "If you are . . ." "if I am . . ." then what?

The great experience of the temptations is the moral and natural outcome of his experience at the baptism. "You are my beloved son" were the words in which Jesus expressed his experience and consciousness of God, rewards of faith. The recorded Satanic attack of "since you are the son of God" reveals a direct challenge to Jesus: how will you make known this fact? This was a natural reaction to the strain and exaltation of his baptism. Evidently the fundamental question in Jesus' mind was the nature of his appeal to those among whom his mission lay. It would appear that Jesus was certain of his "call" to share his own experience of faith. Such experiences of faith, Jesus felt confident, would bring to the expectant, longing multitude the life of peace and security they sought. He also knew what his people expected of the Messiah. To Jesus, intent on following diligently the Will of God, these traditional messianic ideas of his people appeared not as divine inspirations but as Satanic perversions.

Comparing the various accounts, the Matthean order of bread, Temple pinnacle and nations of the world appears to be the more normal and logical development. The following is an attempt to interpret these three temptations.

(i) The temptation to change stones into loaves of bread appears to have come at the close of an extended period of unconscious fasting. "Now that you know that you are the son of God, and thereby possess the creative powers of God, why don't you change these stones into loaves of bread and feed your hungering body?" This was a challenge to his sonship to God. Why not test it out now? Our speculative minds taunt us with the thoughts: if bread, why not drink? if food, why not clothing? if clothing, why not a shelter from the elements? if not for self, why not for friends? if for self, why not for the needy of Nazareth, Galilee, Judea, all Palestine, the whole world? Can it be that this simple temptation involved all these ramifications for Jesus? Probably not, but whether or not it held such connotation for him, one thing is certain; Jesus poignantly answered the temptation with these words: "Man does not live by the acquiring and use of material goods, no matter how badly he may need them. Man lives abundantly only when he feasts upon the intellectual and spiritual sustenance of life." Jesus recognized the temptation as one to do a desirable thing in an undesirable manner. He also realized that to perform any experiments with God was to reveal his uncertainty of God. Trust never desires to tempt, to test or to trifle, but calmly and quietly abides in sure confidence. Thus Jesus thwarted the temptation, and exercised faith.

(ii) The second recorded temptation consisted of the taunt: "Since you yourself are so certain of God, and have such faith in Him, how are you going to prove to others that you are the son of God, the Messiah of Israel, the saviour of mankind? What a reception you would receive, Jesus, if you would appear atop the pinnacle of the Temple and cast your body forth, trusting in God for safe landing, for does not His holy Word declare such protection for His Messiah?" Once again we must assume that Matthew is reporting the traditional statement of Jesus, and therefore the symbols must have some deep significance for Jesus.

Jesus revealed for a second time the same clearness of vision. Revelation comes in a purely spiritual manner; if he himself could learn who he was only by way of spiritual experience, no other way was possible for others. They must come to know him, as he has come to know the Father; and knowing him, they would come to learn what the Kingdom was to be. The old demand for a sign was, for Jesus, just tempting God—putting God to a test which would prove nothing but the doubt and faintheartedness of the one who raised the question. Jesus saw that the way into the Kingdom for himself and for others was the strait and narrow path of spiritual discernment and experience. People could not be coerced into spiritual knowledge.

(iii) The third recorded temptation may have closely followed the second. Jesus was tempted not only to give a sign of his sonship but also to use evil methods of securing all peoples under his influence. The multitudes surging into the Jordan Valley manifested to Jesus the great need of the people for abundant life. If only he could help bring all the nations under the care and inspiration of his heavenly Father . . . It is thrilling to speculate that this temptation was in one sense an evil glorification of his boyhood experience on the hilltop behind his home at Nazareth as he beheld the peoples of the nations plying the caravan route down in the valley to the north. Here, psychologically, Jesus was sitting, except that the mountain had been elevated to a superlative height in order to see even the homelands whence these travelers came. All these should be in his Father's Kingdom, if only he could force them into it.

This temptation is exceedingly strong, in view of the expectant state of his own people. They awaited momentarily the sudden inauguration of the Messianic Age. It was to be one of earthly rule, limited at first to the chosen people of Israel, though ultimately all nations would be invited from the East and the West, the North and the South, to the Holy City in order to pay homage to a Jewish Messiah, God's Anointed. Jesus, once again, saw clearly God's way to bring in the Kingdom. God's method was not compulsion, nor hatred, nor militarism or revolt against Rome, but love, persuasion and the appeal to "changed lives." The Kingdom was God's! He is King. His way alone will bring it in! All men are His children. All men will partake of its blessings, of whatever race, class, nation, creed or sex. This temptation reveals how early in Jesus' ministry the universal character of divine destiny really was.

Thus Jesus faced the implications of his baptismal decision. He faced the decision of giving full time to God in religious service. His ministry was mapped out: it was to be one of "childlike" faith in God; it was to be concerned with the guidance of his people through the narrow gate of spiritual experience. God's Kingdom was spiritual and not materialistic, universal and not provincial; for that was what God had revealed to him in the midst of these temptations. The triumph of Jesus was not in the fact that he *could not* but in that he *did not* sin. His strength came from the belief that God was not to be tested but to be simply trusted and obeyed.

A Crisis
(Matthew 11:20-30)

Scholars may wish to disagree with the implications placed upon the incident of Jesus' upbraiding the Galilean cities. We agree that a gospel is not a biography; we assume the author's intention was to proclaim a faith. Yet embedded in the midst of his sources is definite evidence of a crisis in the preaching ministry of Jesus. Upon the basis of its apparent nature and the context with which it is narrated, it would fit best into the early ministry in Galilee.

The forty days of isolation for meditation are over. The temptations were repulsed, and a trial ministry somewhere in the vicinity of John's Jordan location was under way. Jesus had entered upon his ministry to bring in the Kingdom of God. Then upon the arrest of the Baptist, Jesus changed his locale; he earnestly set forth upon an itinerant ministry back in his home territory of Galilee. Everywhere he spoke crowds gathered. To them he proclaimed his message; with them he shared his faith. Soon he sought companions and converts. From among these he chose twelve men to be his special apostles, first as assistants, then associates, ultimately his agents in the spreading of the "Good News." And what was this "Good News"? It was that the Kingdom of God was at hand, available—now! Men were urged to repent, to lay hold upon the spiritual resources of life from God, and live the life of sonship to Almighty God as Father. As their numbers increased and the new communal life would evolve, they could live in anticipation of that great day not far hence when God would reign over His people in His Kingdom.

Jesus' fame spread far and wide. His mission expanded. Hungering souls were being fed. Then came the moment when Jesus saw his geographical limitations; he could not be everywhere at once. To accelerate his work he sent forth his apostles. We are not sure whether it was merely the Twelve, as according to Mark 6:7 ff., Matthew 10:5 ff., and Luke 9:1 ff., or the seventy(-two), as reported in Luke 10:1 ff. Possibly it was both on many occasions. In faith he sent them forth to share his message of abundant life. He sent them forth not to tell about himself, nor to tell of his own love for them, but to win converts to his way of life: converts who, like the Twelve, had come in some small measure to experience the selfsame joy of eternal life as he had. He recalled that the "second" temptation had taught him how the Kingdom would come only through the narrow gate of personal spiritual experience. Neither Jesus nor his disciples, at first, wished men and women to worship him, but rather only God, the Father. All men were to do the Will of God, not Jesus'. They were to have faith in God, not in him. Only God made eternal life possible in the individual life. Jesus was the saviour, and still is, only in the sense that he has helped to restore men to Life by pointing out the Truth to all, by revealing the Way, and by manifesting the Life that is God's intent for all mankind. Jesus sent forth the messengers two by two. He had great expectations in the results of their ministry. What a disappointment Jesus experienced upon their return.

Luke (10:10–20), in reporting Jesus' disappointment over the experiences of the seventy, may very well have reported what actually happened in the case of the mission of the Twelve, and others. Jesus was dismayed. He had enthusiastically sent them out to spread his gospel, only to discover that he was a bit premature. When they returned, they reflected their delight in what they thought was sweeping success. The thrill and joy which they had experienced in dealing with cases of demon possession was manifested upon their countenances. But they could report no success or give any evidence that the Kingdom of God had taken root as a result of their ministry. Added to the ever-increasing pressure and opposition of the scribes and Pharisees, the deep disappointment at the inadequate results of his messengers caused Jesus to plan and carry out a somewhat "forced" vacation in the area of Tyre and Sidon.

Jesus was faced with the first major crisis of his public ministry. John the Baptist was then dead. Chorazin, Bethsaida and Capernaum lay complacently asleep. Jesus poured out his disappointment upon the cities: "Woe to you, Capernaum, where I have established my mission headquarters! Woe to you, Chorazin and Bethsaida, wherein I am proclaiming deliverance!" But shortly Jesus regained his poise, for the Gospel-writer notes that "in that same hour he rejoiced in the Holy Spirit" (Luke 10:21).

Evidently what he had felt to be God's Will was not. He must acknowledge this fact and strike out on a new path. Here Jesus' faith and insight shine out. He saw two new steps he must take. He must come to a parting of the ways with the old visions of the Kingdom as the prophets saw it, namely, Israel's kingdom. He must take to the path that led out into the unknown; he must accept God's Will that the Kingdom is to be given to this comparative handful of simple folk who alone have had the faith and courage to follow him and to learn from him. The goal was the same: the more adequate preparation of the people for the coming of the Kingdom of God on earth. Only the method has changed.

Though all (Capernaum, Chorazin, Bethsaida, John the Baptist, and his own disciples) had failed to understand his message, Jesus' sense of God's approval carried him on. His faith had conquered once more. Jesus felt that he was still very much alone, tragically so, in his possession of what appeared to be the secret of God's character and will. All others were struggling for it, but he *knew*. Therefore, having seen God's Will for the immediate future, he offered himself to guide those who were willing to learn from him the mystery of the Kingdom, the secret of God's character and will and the nature of life abundant.

Another Crisis—Near Caesarea Philippi
(Mark 8:27–30; cf. Matthew 16:13–20, Luke 9:18–21, John 6:66–69)

The next crisis in Jesus' ministry took place near the northern city of Caesarea Philippi. Following the first crisis, Jesus had taken his followers into the territory of Tyre and Sidon, where he undertook to develop in profound detail his divinely inspired message that he believed would bring in the Kingdom of God. In daily fellowship with some twenty-five of his most intimate disciples (i.e., add to the Twelve those other disciples mentioned in Luke 8:3*b* and Acts 1:21–26), Jesus went into a rather detailed exposition of his Good News as to the meaning and character of the Kingdom and of life eternal. At this time Jesus undoubtedly shared with his followers his most intimate experiences of God and Life: e.g., his baptism and his temptation experience. The records of subsequent events indicate that it was about from this time in their experience that they knew of intimate spiritual experiences of Jesus. One illustration will suffice to indicate what is meant here. The disciples' report of the Transfiguration includes the detail that a voice out of heaven utters the identical words which Jesus had reported as coming to him at the moment of baptism. Psychologically, this was as it should have been, assuming that not many days before Jesus had related his story of the occasion by the Jordan. This, however, is getting ahead of the present story.

We have no documentation as to the length of this sojourn near Tyre and Sidon, but Jesus concluded what he deemed sufficient training for his intimate disciples and dismissed them. What follows in the Gospel record appears to indicate that he sent them ahead of himself to visit their separate homes with the specific instruction to listen to any hearsay regarding his work. They were to congregate at a specified spot to the northeast of the Sea of Galilee. Upon his arrival at this designated location, however, he was given an unexpected enthusiastic reception by some four thousand friends and devotees. After a seemingly miraculous feeding of the multitudes, he extricated himself from the crowd and slipped away toward Caesarea Philippi in the neighboring tetrarchy. When his intimate followers rejoined him as he neared the new Herodian capital, he carefully prepared himself to meet a "second" crisis.

It is interesting to note in the first three Gospels that Jesus hardly ever directed the attention of his disciples to himself, save for the command to follow him. This was perfectly natural and normal, and perfectly proper and correct, for Jesus desired that they look *with* him, not *at* him. He did not tell them who he was, or ask them what they thought about him, but kept them God-centered and gospel-centered in their entire outlook and faith.

Now, however, he apparently felt compelled to sound them out in regard to himself and his ministry among them. From his baptism, or an early period in his public ministry, he recognized that in his knowledge and experience of God and His Kingdom he seemed to stand out alone in human experience. He perceived that as a result of this constant companionship with God he was gradually taking on some of the attributes and attitudes of His Heavenly Father. Through such intimate relationship with God he had come to know and understand God far better and more deeply than anyone else. In order for his disciples to discern this special relationship of sonship to God as Father, they too must have such close relationship with God in their own lives and experiences. It is psychologically true that to appreciate and recognize anything spiritual or of value in the spiritual realm, there must be some common ground and some qualitative likeness on the part of the observer. Therefore, Jesus asked his intimate disciples some rather startling questions: "Who do men say that I am?" and "Who do you say that I am?" If both questions were answered in identical terms, then Jesus would know that his disciples were not really ready to advance with him to the next step in the bringing in of the Kingdom of God.

The first question, "Who do men say that I am?" was answered correctly, as Jesus expected: "Just another prophet." But to the second question, "Who do you think I am?" the impetuous Peter blurted out, "Why, you are the Messiah!" Jesus was elated. Peter in a flash of insight and high spiritual attainment had "seen" the reflection of the Godhead in the character of Jesus. To Peter, Jesus must be God's anointed, the Messiah, the one who would bring in the Kingdom. Peter saw in Jesus the character of God lived out among men. Yet Peter was still a Jew, a monotheist, who would have been horrified at any suggestion that would have denied that "the Lord Thy God is One God." Nevertheless, Peter saw God reflected in Jesus and had the courage to say so. This was the answer that Jesus undoubtedly had hoped for. He wanted all men to be like himself, true images of God, the Father. This *was* the beginning of the bringing in of the Kingdom, for here were *sons,* at least two, Jesus and Peter.

Jesus was overjoyed! The moment of vindication had come. His faith in the methods of God was beginning to get results; God's way of establishing the new humanity and the new social order was bearing fruit. This surely was the way God had intended to bring in the new era of righteousness and peace, and not by any catastrophic appearance of a heavenly creature descending on clouds of glory in some miraculous manner. Here was one, Peter, who, unforced and walking by the same quiet way which Jesus himself had traversed, had learned the secret of abundant life and could thereby recognize it in others.

Jesus was right when he is reported as replying: "Blessed are you, Simon Bar-Jona! For flesh and blood has not revealed this to you, but my Father who is in heaven" (Matthew 16:17). The soul and mind of earth-bound, materialistic Simon, concerned with flesh and blood, had certainly not made it possible for him to come to this conclusion. Rather, it was God, the Father in heaven, who had flashed upon the mind and soul of a spiritually sensitive Simon the realization of this great reality: Jesus is the Messiah! Peter was on sufficiently high moral and spiritual ground to receive the revelation and comprehend it.

We read in Scripture (Genesis 32:24–31) how Jacob's name was changed to Israel because, having wrestled with God all night, he came out of the struggle a new person. So now Jesus recognized in Simon the marks of a similar personal transformation, and changed his name to Peter (Matthew 16:18). Here was one, Simon, who had been brought to such a spiritual level of development that he recognized the very nature of Jesus in his full manhood. As he had recognized the divine quality of Jesus' character, so Jesus replied by indicating the divine quality of Peter's character.

By Peter's confession, Jesus' faith in God and His Way had been rewarded by a companion on that Way, by an associate in the sharing of the "good news." What Peter had confessed, the rest of his intimate disciples must feel, so Jesus reasoned. Through faith Jesus had attained his goal. His "second" crisis was passed: the crisis of whether or not the way of education of, companionship with and exemplification to this small handful of disciples was the way God meant His Kingdom to take root and grow.

In confronting this crisis, Jesus had arrived at the place where God's way was sufficiently clear to him to set his mind at rest about the future of the Kingdom. Two glimpses of truth apparently came surging in upon him. Somehow God was calling him to be the true Messiah. Furthermore, Jesus saw his prophetic vision of a community of people possessing the real character of God and obedient to His Will.

Just how long Jesus had been coming to the point of realizing his Messiahship, rather than the role of a mere leader of a people seeking abundant life, we cannot be sure. If the primacy

The Faith He Experienced

of Mark is held and this record is trusted as historic fact, the confession of Peter is the first definite and distinct messianic moment in Jesus' life. Matthew and Luke appear to have attempted a psychological anticipation by presenting Jesus as aware of his messiahship throughout his ministry, if not his whole life. Yet it would appear that it was actually at this moment in Caesarea Philippi that Simon confronted Jesus for the first time with the messianic issue. It would appear that simultaneously, Jesus, in pondering the messianic prophesies in the holy Scriptures, had come to ally himself in some way to the Suffering Servant of Isaiah. Could it be that Jesus reasoned that he was that Suffering Servant? Circumstances up to that point seemed to warrant the thought. Dared he think it? Yes, he did. The rest of his life fell into harmonious agreement with the vision of Isaiah. Well did he recall that Sabbath day in Nazareth when he had preached from that sacred scroll (Luke 4:16 ff.). Although Isaiah's concept involved a people, Israel, to live out the part of the Suffering Servant, God's Will for Jesus was to fulfill in a personal way that ancient prophecy.

Jesus also saw with more nearly perfected insight the true God-intended concept of His Kingdom: he saw in Peter's confession a new foundation for the rising new community, the true Israel. It would be a community of people possessing the characteristics of God and being obedient to His Will. The word translated "church" in this Matthean passage (Matthew 16:18, cf. 18:18) is probably a reflection of the period of Gospel-writing. Jesus probably used an Aramaic word better translated into English by the word "assembly" or "congregation." This "congregation" was to be comprised of God-like persons like Peter and himself; the spiritual methods chosen by God at the time of the temptation were vindicated. It had also become increasingly clear that this spiritual way meant a divergence of immense importance from the Jewish national hope. Jesus had held this Jewish national hope, also, at first, but God had revealed to him a higher concept of the Kingdom and more excellent means to establish the spiritual community. Jesus' faith in God and in His Will had rewarded him with the vision of the true nature of the Kingdom. He now saw for the first time that forwarding God's Kingdom in this new way meant opposition, persecution, even death; and he began to speak of it. But as has been noted, as he confronted this crisis the confession of Peter helped Jesus to set his mind at rest about the future of his divine mission. Here were others who had the same level of perception, and ever-growing spirits to match it.

The Transfiguration
(Mark 9:2–13, Matthew 17:1–13, Luke 9:28–36)

It would appear that the Gospel-writers regarded the story of the Transfiguration as merely another evidence of Jesus' divinity. Some scholars have gone to great length to discredit the story; some have even classified it as a misplaced resurrection legend. Even some of those who have accepted it as historical have suggested that it should be placed before the confession of Peter. When the Transfiguration, however, is linked with the visit to the territory of Tyre and Sidon, and with the possible sharing at that time of Jesus' experiences of baptism and temptation, one can see a very comprehensible pattern of experience come into view. When the Transfiguration is connected vitally, as in the text, with the confession of Peter, one finds the Transfiguration the natural and normal consequence of the new knowledge gained en route to Caesarea Philippi.

It would appear that the "second" crisis of his ministry was the turning point for Jesus. Up to now, Jesus was courageously fulfilling his calling: bringing people through repentance and reception of a newness of life each to his individual sonship to the Heavenly Father and social responsibility in the new community. Step by step Jesus discovered God's Will by choosing the higher road, the higher set of values in life. At last, upon the confession of Peter, Jesus saw the path that lay ahead of him a little more clearly than he had ever seen it before. As he grew in God-consciousness and became more certain of God's Will for himself, the plan of life that God had laid out for him came more and more distinctly into focus. He saw now that it meant carrying on the work of establishing the Kingdom by means of education and the exemplary life. This entailed carrying the "good news" to the nerve center of Judaism, Jerusalem. He also realized, on the basis of past opposition and persecution, that it meant almost certain death if he remained steadfast to the Divine Will and Way as he now saw it and if he failed to compromise with the representatives of Judaism. It was now up to him to accept or reject the almost certain death sentence. In complete faith to God, he willingly accepted.

One week had passed before the real significance of the momentous occasion of Peter's confession crystallized. Jesus took his three most intimate disciples, Peter, James and John, and went up into a mountain to pray. It was there that the significance of Peter's confession really dawned upon the three men. It was there in prayer that Jesus came to the full realization of his mission in life and its cost. Oh, the thrill of it—the challenge of it—the relative certainty that he was actually on the path of God's Will for his life! Such joy, peace, power, hope he experienced that night after communing with His Heavenly Father. His whole disposition, attitude of life and outlook on life took on a new quality. Whatever we may wish to call it (whether cosmic consciousness, possession by the Holy Spirit, the incarnation of God, or the Kingdom of God within a man), Jesus realized the fullness of life as he had never experienced it before. He had submitted his life in faith to God, and as a result had participated in the good life in all its divinely intended quality. God had richly blessed him. God had rewarded him for his faith, love and obedience. Jesus was experiencing man's fullest maturity, a quality which seemed to set him apart from his fellows.

His three companions were to no less a degree coming alive not only to the true nature of Jesus and his message but also to the whole meaning of life itself. In their ecstasy they thought they saw God in Jesus; they believed that they were experiencing the fulfillment of God's promises proclaimed by the prophets of old. When they beheld the "transfigured" Jesus, they envisioned his purity and relative perfectness in what they later described as his "glistening" appearance. They believed they saw him speaking with Elijah, the symbol for the prophets, and with Moses, the symbol of the Torah. They described their moving experience ever afterwards in these tremendous symbols.

Out of this great experience was born an idea that was difficult for the disciples of Jesus to cast off. Somehow the disciples' worship and love of God became erroneously and unfortunately channeled into the love of God's reflection in their Master, Jesus. In their zeal to worship, Jesus became more real than God. Henceforth they considered Jesus eternally superior and prior to themselves, not alone in degree but in substance, to use the terminology of later Christian theology. He was no longer a mere master, the foremost companion, but was God's special representative and ultimately the very incarnation of God Himself. From that moment the idea of a Christ-centered religion grew until it became established as Christianity. Somehow the life-changing faith Jesus sought to share with mankind became lost. The "good news" of a loving heavenly Father who cared for His children as Father for son, and the "congregation" of sons of God as the true nature of the Kingdom of God, was the message Jesus brought to mankind. Jesus' gospel was God-centered; that of his disciples henceforth even to this day is Christ-centered. The truly power-ladened word of life, however, is that gospel which Jesus brought into the world—no matter how important the Church's gospel *about* Jesus may be.

From this moment onward, Jesus set his face steadfastly toward Jerusalem. He was certain in his own soul that it was now God's Will that he should go to the Holy City and place before the officials of Israel and of the faith the words of Life that he had to share.

The Resurrection in the Faith of Jesus
(Mark 9:30–32, Matthew 17:22–23, Luke 9:43*b*–45)

The resurrection is not often approached from the side of Jesus' experience. We usually consider the question pertaining to the risen Jesus as a part of the faith-experience of his more intimate disciples. It is rarely thought of as affecting Jesus' personal experience at all. Somehow our minds have dwelt largely on the experience of the disciples in professing that Jesus was raised from the grave, as he prophesied. From that vantage point we seek to construct our theology on the matter of resurrection and immortality. But like Job (14:14), like all mankind, Jesus also asked the eternal question, "If a man die, shall he live again?"

It was during the fast-moving events which took place near Caesarea Philippi that Jesus first mentioned the subject of resurrection. This was the logical place for it in his experience, and the Gospel record so places it; for it was a by-product of those experiences. Jesus came to see that his life led to death if he held fast to his faith in God. He had accepted, from the Father, the cost of confidence and loyalty. With the certainty of death came the certainty of the resurrection. And both of these certainties came from a supreme expression of faith. If, however, Jesus had had any foreknowledge of his own resurrection, then his hope would not have been the ultimate expression of his faith in God.

As he accepted the new challenge and entered into the conflict not only with the religious authorities of his time but with the zealous leaders of political rebellion, decisions of forcing God to bring in the Kingdom grew stronger. Yet his faith in God likewise increased to match the challenge. Death appeared nevertheless to be inevitable. And it is in such times of stress that the hope of justice and vindication seeks its satisfaction in the hope of resurrection, or immortality. This was true in the trying times of Antiochus Epiphanes, which produced the scriptural book of Daniel; it was true also in the difficult days of Caesar Domitian, when the Apocalypse of John was written. So, now, it was true in the experience of Jesus himself. This was not the time for further doubt and hesitancy. It was the time for courage and stout-hearted determination to see his mission through to completion, whatever the cost. It was an opportunity for faith. In such steps of faith he had had much experience. God had vindicated every step up to this point. Jesus must now take the most daring step of faith yet known in the history of man's relationship to his God. He must trust God through Death to Life Immortal.

The belief was already held in Jewish circles that the righteous dead, the saints and martyrs of old, were to rise again to share the blessings of the earthly Divine Kingdom in the day of its glory. This was Jewish intellectual belief. Jesus, however, having found God always trustworthy, once again surrendered himself completely to the belief in the resurrection. Such was his daring "childlike" faith in God.

A Further Crisis

(Mark 11:1–15:8, Matthew 21:1–28:20, Luke 19:29–24:52)

The Passion narrative appears to be the oldest written account of Jesus' life, and was recorded, probably, before his "sayings" were. Therefore, we have every reason to trust the account for historic accuracy. In fact, the narrative brings to fruition that spiritual journey which the other, later-written accounts intimate was the experience of Jesus.

As Jesus came down to the Holy City, he saw that it was as though he were entering some labyrinthine canyon. The towering walls of opposition on both sides caused it to grow darker and darker as the way grew more narrow and serious. No outlet was visible, but the soul of Jesus cried out, "There must be a way out. There is a way out, if God is God." He staked everything on the faithfulness of God. As God had entrusted him with

The Faith He Experienced

a message of abundant living, so he must trust God as he drew near to the final crisis of his ministry, and of his life.

Jesus had begun his ministry with a profound spiritual experience. His relationship to God and the Kingdom was fully revealed to him. Upon the reality of that experience he had staked everything. He had experienced the "first" crisis. Suffering general rejection and disappointment in his Galilean ministry, he accepted it in full faith from the Father's Hand. He had heard of John's death, and had seen no intervention of God for him. From experience Jesus drew God's token for himself, that he, Jesus, must also suffer at the hands of the authorities. All through his ministry there was an increasing sense of divergence between the nature of the Kingdom and the Messiah as it was revealed to him and that which the people round about him expected. For Jesus, the Kingdom was not to be a materialistic political one, but a spiritual Kingdom. The Messiah was not to be a reigning triumphant potentate, but a suffering compassionate servant of the people. Gradually he realized how much tradition would have to go.

The crisis broke after the Last Supper with his disciples in the upper room of Mary's (Mark's) home in Jerusalem. As he saw Judas leave the table and depart from the gathering, he realized what a messiah executed as a common criminal was going to mean for all patriotic hopes, all Jewish dreams of freedom and an earthly kingdom. But God's Will was best. God's destiny would unfold. He was sure of that. But did he have sufficient faith to measure up to the crisis? He went out into the solitude of the garden of Gethsemane to fight another lonely battle in agony.

In the garden Jesus took Peter, James and John apart from the rest of his intimate disciples to a quiet spot to pray. He had taken these three with him to this inner sanctuary of his spiritual life before. Perhaps he considered these three men closest to his level of spiritual life and discernment. He needed not only their moral support but their spiritual presence in this hour of supreme faith. Jesus sought their sympathy as he prepared to face the crisis, "the cup," which he warned them they too some day would taste. The temptation came upon him to take the easier road and thereby to doubt and disobey God. It was still possible to withdraw, to step away quietly into exile, while his companions slept, to avoid what became the final crisis. But what if he had? Three times he faced the awful choice; three times he felt himself shrinking from the cup, yet with resolute faith he stretched forth his hands to grasp it, for it was his Father's Will. He sought some reasonable answer, but only the sense of inner assurance came upon him that this was the only way—it was God's Way.

Jesus had hoped that all those "burdened and heavy-ladened" would learn from him the way of life which would restore them to abundant living. Only a handful had the faith to follow. The Father's Will now appeared to be that he should die an ignominious death to save them as well as himself. For Jesus to veer from doing God's Will at this fatal moment would have been to experience a greater death than a martyr's physical demise. The prophecy of Isaiah 53 seemed to be fulfilling itself in history—although we must point out that this passage was never considered messianic by the Jews, nor did Isaiah expect his words to be personified in one person, but rather in a nation, Israel.

Jesus' childlike faith triumphed; and he said: "Father, if you are willing, remove this 'cup' from me: nevertheless, not my will, but yours, be done" (Luke 22:42).

On the Cross

(Mark 15:21–41, Matthew 27:32–56, Luke 23:26–49, John 19:17–30)

The fatal hour came. The critical observer that day waited to see how Jesus' faith would measure up to the ordeal. Would he be able to maintain the sincere childlike faith in the Father that he had been preaching and practicing during his public ministry? What would be Jesus' faith on the cross? The answers

The Faith He Experienced   51

to these questions hang on the interpretation and value placed upon the one great cry on the cross, "My God, my God, why hast thou forsaken me?" (Mark 15:34.) One must know in what sense and under what motivations Jesus uttered these historic words, whose very utterance remained indelibly upon the ears of his followers. *Eloi, Eloi, lama sabach-thani?* rang forever in their ears, as is evidenced by their inclusion in the Gospel records some forty years later. In what sense did Jesus utter them? Did Jesus cry out in sincere expression of his own soul's anguish? Or did he seek to sublimate his anguish in song, perhaps accidentally selecting a very appropriate Psalm? Or did he deliberately seek to express the deep conviction of his soul in that Psalm which above all others expressed his plight and faith in final victory? Or could it have been the garbled report of the bystanders (cf. Mark 15:35) placed side by side with a Psalm which, the infant church later discovered, described the plight and circumstances of their Master's final days so uncannily?

In attempting to reconstruct the actual experience, let us review the workings of Jesus' mind up to this moment. He had chosen, step by step, what he felt was God's Way and Will for his life and mission, and the vindications had come. At last he realized that it led even unto death, and in the agony of Gethsemane, he surrendered his life in total abandonment to God's Will, though his own will and mind sought a way out. Agony filled his soul in the garden. Then came the arrest, the trials, the scourgings, the march to Golgotha, and finally he found himself upon a cross between two others.

Still, through the mockery of the "trials," and the heartless jibes of the religious leaders at his supposed Messiahship, he clung to the possibility that the Father might intervene in some way. But his strength was waning, and there did not appear any sign in the darkness which was coming over the land. All hopes were on the precipice of despair. Although in Gethsemane Jesus saw that God's Will was that he should die, he hoped. The end drew near, and the passionate cry of broken-hearted disappointment broke forth from his lips: *Eloi, Eloi, lama sabach-thani?* (Mark 15:34 and Matthew 27:46.) It reveals that the final agony was not of the body but of the mind.

This is the only recorded occasion where Jesus addressed God as God. Yet it appears highly probable that these were the actual words, as evidenced by the fact that the saying has been preserved supposedly in the exact Aramaic words of Jesus. The Psalm, however, was written in Hebrew, and read and sung in that language. It would appear, therefore, that probably it was not a mere recitation on the part of Jesus but an expression of his own experience, though having some psychological connection with the Twenty-second Psalm.

The cry of anguish was uttered or sung. The supreme moment of conflict passed. Faith in the Father came welling back to Jesus. The words came, apparently with a force and strength that astonished the onlookers: "Father, into thy hands I commit my spirit!" (Luke 23:46.) This was a cry of victory.

Jesus accepted the issue of the cross with all its finality and apparently set his mind and heart at peace. He saw the finite unalterability of the situation on the one side and the infinite possibilities when placed at the Father's disposal on the other side. It might be resurrection; it must be vindication. As a child he had found himself at home in the Father's House, the Jerusalem Temple. Now he entrusted his spirit, having done all, to the Father's hands in faith. The rest was up to the Father.

CHAPTER IV

THE FAITH HE LIVED

A man is known not only by the great moments of his life experiences but by the insignificant acts which also express his faith, yet ofttimes pass before the public eye unscrutinized. This was as true of Jesus as of anyone else. Historically, Christians as well as unbelievers have been interested more in what Jesus said than how he responded to life-situations. The earliest records, oral and written, were concerned chiefly with reporting his sayings. This was the aim of our Gospel-writers. Yet imbedded in their accounts are significant reflections unwittingly recorded by the authors. It is with these less significant actions that we shall deal in this chapter in order to discover other aspects of Jesus' personal faith and beliefs.

In Regard to His Own Family

Jesus appears to have been the first-born of Mary. The children who followed, evidently in somewhat quick succession, form a sizable family of at least nine members, if not as many as twelve. Despite Roman Catholic teaching to the contrary, Jesus appears to have had four brothers whose names are known (Mark 6:3 and Matthew 13:55) and at least two sisters. What evidence we have points to a very harmonious family up to the moment when Jesus felt led to enter upon his public preaching ministry. Just when Joseph died we cannot ascertain; the evidence is that he was alive when Jesus was twelve and that he had been dead some time when Jesus was "about thirty" (Luke 3:23). It has been suggested that this was the reason why Jesus was rather late in entering upon his public ministry. This need not be so (cf. Matthew 19:12). Jesus, however, according to Jewish custom, appears to have followed in Joseph's footsteps as a carpenter and as head of the household.

These facts show the sense of responsibility towards his family which Jesus apparently had until that moment when he permitted himself to be baptized at the hands of John the Baptist. From that time forward he appears to have severed himself from that responsibility—in fact, actually demanding similar action on the part of others (cf. Mark 10:29–30, Matthew 19:29, Luke 18:29–30). We have already seen that tendency taking shape in Jesus' life as early as the age of twelve (Luke 2:41–52), when he gave his first loyalty to God and His Kingdom. It would appear that when this severance finally occurred his family regarded it as unnatural of him and reluctantly regarded him as "beside himself" (Mark 3:21, cf. John 7:5). Eventually they took definite steps to reclaim him and to bring him back into the family circle (Mark 3:31–35, Matthew 12:46–50, Luke 8:19–21), but to no avail. It was on this latter occasion that Jesus expounded his concept of universal brotherhood. In the recorded form, the words Jesus used in regard to his family seem rather harsh. We must not believe, however, that Jesus had forsaken them; he simply felt dedicated to a higher loyalty than the family unit.

Jesus also believed that such a higher loyalty was God's Will for all men (Mark 10:29–30, Matthew 19:29, Luke 18:29–30). Jesus felt very much a part of all mankind; he was not bound by any blood relationship. This was due not to any supernormal or supernatural aspect of his being but to his real human sense of world citizenship. Aware that circumstances have placed him in time, space, race, creed and linguistic grouping, a true son of God never feels a part of any one of these categories. Jesus believed that this sense of world citizenship within the individual soul was the basis of healthy human relationships and of the Kingdom of God. Only when one is consciously bound by ties of race, class or creed do animosity, selfishness, pride and prejudice arise. Jesus lived above all these tensions and dissensions, and expected the same experience for all mankind, because he believed that was God's intent. Because Jesus so lived, the world has been unable to make any classification other than divinity for him. Each race, each nationality of mankind, has thought of Jesus as belonging in universal terms to its particular group. Therefore, we see Jesus' faith in a humanity made worthy of his brotherhood. This he would have us imitate, not in any hypocritical fashion, but in a genuine expression of our experience like unto his.

In Regard to His Rivals

The use of the phrase "his rivals" is not in keeping with Jesus' attitude toward his contemporaries. Yet the term is thought essential for clarification and classification. During his ministry Jesus had two specific "rivals": John the Baptist and the unknown exorcist (Mark 9:38–41, Luke 9:49–50). As we study his relationship with these two contemporaries, we shall discover further aspects of his faith in mankind. And from him we learn.

In regard to his strongest "rival," Jesus had the greatest admiration and praise: "among those born of women there has arisen no one greater than John the Baptist" (Matthew 11:11a, cf. Luke 7:28). The early church could not agree with Jesus at this point. John had too strong a personality. Evidence shows that the movement which grew out of his preaching by the Jordan River continued for several centuries; the sect was such a strong contender with Christianity at the turn of the second century (A.D. 100) that the writer of the Fourth Gospel appears called upon to take drastic action in recording John's relation to Jesus. The Church could not blot out the fact that Jesus was baptized by John; yet the Church refused to allow John equal status with Jesus. According to the ideas of the Church, Jesus was the Messiah. The Scriptures had prophesied that Elijah must return to prepare the way for the coming of the Messiah. Therefore, John must be that forerunner and nothing more. John's disciples refused to accept this status for their leader. Such a controversy never entered the mind or feelings of Jesus. As far as Jesus was concerned, John had inaugurated the gospel message: "Repent, for the kingdom of heaven is at hand" (Matthew 3:2). Jesus merely picked up that proclamation at the moment of his return from the wilderness temptation and developed it according to his own understanding of God's intention (Matthew 4:17). For Jesus it was the call not for the destruction of the morally unfit, but for the restoration of all mankind to moral health. Nevertheless, he rejoiced in the fact that each in his own way could assist God in restoring abundant life to mankind. John was ascetic; Jesus was social. John expected the people to come to him; Jesus went to the people. Yet they both demanded confession and repentance in the sense of re-thinking, of attaining new attitudes of and toward life. As a consequence a whole new humanity would be developed. This was John's, Jesus' and God's chief concern for mankind. Therefore, why regard each as a "rival"? Each was rather a contemporary working toward common ends.

When we turn to the incident of the unnamed sorcerer (Mark 9:38-41, Luke 9:49-50), we find a similar situation present. The fiery sons of Zebedee were furious upon their return from a preaching mission because an unknown exorcist was threatening the prestige of the disciples' work, and possibly Jesus'. John bar Zebedee would have liked to see the stranger absorbed into Jesus' fellowship and thus lose his popularity. Yet we notice that Jesus' attitude toward the exorcist was quite different.

What the phrase "in your name" (Mark 9:38, Luke 9:49) may mean we are not certain. Could it be that this was an unbaptized disciple of Jesus working in his own way to help establish God's Kingdom, and perhaps to add to the glory of Jesus? This is what Mark thought it meant (9:39). May the phrase "in your name" not mean, however, "in your spirit," i.e., "like you"? If this be the proper interpretation, then we have another sensitive soul accompanying John and Jesus in seeking to emphasize the moral life in contrast to pharisaic emphasis upon ceremonial correctness. The usual reaction to such a contemporary would be that of jealousy, as displayed by John bar Zebedee. For Jesus, however, this stranger was no rival: "Do not forbid him; for he that is not against you is for you" (Luke 9:50, Mark 9:40). Here was another instance of unity in the spirit. The exorcist was unknown to Jesus and his disciples; yet, because he was seeking to do that which Jesus regarded as God's Will, the exorcist was not to be feared but assisted or let alone. Such a wholesome spirit and attitude Jesus had. Jesus would have his disciples share it with him.

Thus we see that Jesus' faith in mankind is one of trust and respect. One's fellow man is not to be feared or discounted, snubbed or made to feel inferior, subordinated, or exploited. Rather, he is to be encouraged and assisted. The attitude is definitely altruistic rather than egoistic, concerned with causes rather than with personal gain, limitless in scope instead of being confined to self-interest.

In Regard to His Contemporaries

When we study Jesus' reactions to his contemporaries, we discover a similar set of attitudes and responses. Jesus' first response to a crowd was one of compassion (Mark 6:34, Matthew 14:14). He loved people, especially children (Mark 10:13–16, Luke 18:15–17, Matthew 19:13–15), who are of limitless delight to him (cf. Matthew 11:17, Luke 7:32). It is reported that he looked upon the rich young man and "loved him" (Mark 10:21a). Jesus always reveled in the presence of personalities with potentialities, and the small child usually served as his object lesson (Mark 9:36, Matthew 18:4, Luke 9:47–48). Evidently this was Jesus' usual approach to people. Let us look for a moment, however, at several of the particular groups with which Jesus was forced by circumstances to deal. There were the publicans and sinners, the handicapped (i.e., physically, mentally and morally), people of other races, governmental officials, and women and children.

Almost from the very beginning of Jesus' ministry he was criticized for having fellowship with publicans and sinners. The publicans were the collaborators of the day, native Jews willing to serve the Empire in preference to the nationalism of their own people. Matthew (Levi) was a publican (Mark 2:13–14, Matthew 9:9, Luke 5:27). So was Zacchaeus (Luke 19:1–10). Jesus sympathized with their lot so much that he dared to make a publican the hero of one of his parables (Luke 18:10–14). Socially ostracized, the publicans were relatively friendless. Yet Jesus said, in effect: these are children of God like the rest of us; these are our neighbors as much as those whom we know and respect; these deserve brotherly treatment just as much as our dearest friends.

The sinners, so-called, were "those poor in spirit" known as the *am-ha-aretz* (i.e., those of the land, the peasants). Primarily thought of in religious rather than economic terms, they were regarded as "sinners." Unable economically, socially and religiously to maintain the strict letter of the Torah in a fashion worthy of pharisaic recognition, they allowed themselves to become callous through continuing some semblance of piety. Jesus likewise sympathized with their lot. In fact, he felt that he was more akin to them than to the Pharisees. His message, his way of life, was tuned to their level of life and attainment. The common people heard him gladly. Jesus said, "Those who are well have no need of a physician, but those who are sick; I came not to call the righteous, but sinners." (Mark 2:17.) Luke adds significant words, "to repentance" (Luke 5:32). Jesus was calling sinners not to further social revelry but to new life. We are not to infer from these words of Jesus that he regarded the Pharisees healthy but rather that he was here to help those who were aware of their needs. He could not help the bigoted and conceited members of the human family; only the pliable and teachable ones. With these he preferred to have fellowship.

A second group of slighted people were the handicapped in body, mind and spirit. Ever conscious of the significance of his second temptation in the wilderness (no miracles for miracles'

The Faith He Lived   59

sake), Jesus was hesitant to assist until the individual made the first approach. This was undoubtedly necessary for a cure to take place. Always he commended the person on his great faith (cf. Mark 5:34, Luke 8:48, Matthew 9:22); his failure to perform miracles appears to rest upon the lack of such faith (Mark 6:6a, Matthew 13:58). Jesus' compassion went out to these people who, invalids for the most part because of forces beyond their control, found it all but impossible to live the free, full and wholesome life of a child of God. God had not planned it so. Jesus was more fortunate than they. He had discovered his power to help, and he used it where sincere faith was ever present. His love of people radiated even upon these poor souls. The blind (Mark 10:46-52, Matthew 20:29-34, Luke 18:35-43), the lepers (Mark 1:40-45, Matthew 8:2-4, Luke 5:12-16), the insane (Mark 5:1-20, Matthew 8:28-34, Luke 8:26-39), the immoral (Luke 7:37; cf. Mark 14:3-9, Matthew 26:6-13; also John 7:3, 8:11 spurious, and 12:1-8), all felt the touch of his friendly hand and spirit (Matthew 15:29-31).

Then there were the foreigners with whom Jesus came in contact: the Roman centurion (Matthew 8:5-13, Luke 7:1-10), the Syro-Phoenician woman (Mark 7:24-30, Matthew 15:21-28), the Samaritans (Luke 9:51-56) and the Greeks (John 12:20-21), just to list a few. There are only two instances when Jesus appears to be provincial; in each case it may have been for the sake of expediency. The first is in Jesus' advice to his disciples as he sends them forth (Matthew 10:5b-6): "Go nowhere among the Gentiles, and enter no town of the Samaritans, but go rather to the lost sheep of the house of Israel." As his own ministry canceled this specific instruction, it is reasonable to suspect that Jesus had a reason for such advice—that they should begin their ministry among people with whom they have some rapport, and then enter into a difficult field of service and there test their faith and message. The other case is in connection with the trip to Tyre and Sidon, where the Syro-Phoenician woman recognized Jesus (Mark 7:24-30, Matthew 15:21-28). It would appear that Jesus sought to act the part of a typically prejudiced Jew of his day, but without success. Her persistence disgruntled his disciples, but softened his heart, and he yielded to his fundamental motives of friendliness and service and did what she bid him to do. On every occasion Jesus appears to treat all persons alike, regardless of race, tongue, nationality or class. To each man in his need Jesus gave his best efforts, and he expected no less from his followers.

Among the duties and loyalties of men, those to the community are the most demanding at times. Sometimes the community requires an individual loyalty superior to that required by a man's family, his wife or himself, especially in time of communal danger. Thus we are eager to investigate the place of government among the loyalties of Jesus. This we can best discover in his dealings with government officials and in his attitude toward his personal responsibility to that government in the form of tribute.

The earliest reference to Jesus responding to a government official is the occasion when he called Herod Antipas "that fox" (Luke 13:31–33). The account indicates that Jesus felt perfectly safe, for whoever heard of a prophet dying outside of Jerusalem? This account may have been edited in the light of actual history, but it undoubtedly reflects the attitude and courage of Jesus toward a political dictator. Jesus felt perfectly safe, for were not the people on his side? And were not the people they who make or break rulers?

The second occasion when Jesus faced governmental power was in connection with his trials. At that time Jesus first faced the "quisling" deputies of his day, that Jewish ecclesiastical hierarchy which depended upon Roman prestige for power (Mark 14:53–55, Matthew 26:57–68, Luke 22:54,63–71, John 18:12–13,19–24). In the face of illegal questioning, Jesus maintained his poise and calm in silence (Mark 14:61a, Matthew 26:63a). Only at last, when the high priest appears to have solemnly pleaded with Jesus to admit or deny his Messiahship, did Jesus answer, and then with an unequivocal affirmative. Evidently

The Faith He Lived

Jesus regarded all the legal maneuvering as so much interesting waste of time, the practice of pure mechanics according to the letter of the Torah rather than the spirit of it. The hierarchy appeared to be the final religious authority in this life, but Jesus knew better. God was ruler yet. "And do not fear those who kill the body but cannot kill the soul" (Matthew 10:28, cf. Luke 12:4), he had once told his listeners. Now he lived according to that saying.

When he was brought before Pontius Pilate, the Roman procurator of Judea, Jesus continued to maintain his poise and calm in silence (Mark 15:5, Matthew 27:14; cf. John 19:9-11). Luke (13:31-33) is the only Gospel writer to relate Jesus' appearance before Herod Antipas, "that fox." According to the record (Luke 23:8), Herod Antipas had never seen Jesus before this moment; this appears strange but probable. Here, once again, Jesus remained silent, realizing, perhaps, that lack of common understanding made talk futile. This was one lesson Stephen, at his trial, failed to learn from his master (Acts 7:1,2). When placed before the same tribunal, Stephen proceeded to take advantage of the opportunity to argue, to plead; hopefully he sought to convert his hearers. With deeper insight and acumen, Jesus saw the uselessness of such procedure, knowing that the verdict in such a case rested solely upon the judgment of the one in final authority at the moment. Thus we see that Jesus' faith appeared to rest in God, rather than in men.

In regard to Jesus' sense of citizenship-responsibility we have two major instances of tribute-paying. First, we can be sure that as a sincere Jew he paid what he believed was God's due and more. In fact, Peter admits that Jesus is a faithful Temple-tax payer (Matthew 17:24,25). Matthew alone records this incident in the Master's life. After an extended absence in the vicinities of Tyre, Sidon and Caesarea Philippi, the Temple-tax collector appeared at the home of Simon Peter when Jesus and his disciples returned to Capernaum after the Transfiguration. In regard to Jesus' attitude as reflected in this incident, one comes to the conclusion that Jesus felt morally and spiritually free from all responsibility to the Temple organization, yet for the sake of harmony he gave (Matthew 17:27).

The other responsibility as a citizen of that day was to the Empire. The Pharisees and Herodians confronted Jesus with this question on his day of teaching during the last week (Matthew 22:17, Mark 2:14, Luke 20:22). The Zealots regarded payment of this tax as unpatriotic and unlawful. But once again we see Jesus' attitude and faith expressed in a very succinct saying which has become world-famous, yet is rarely understood: "Render to Caesar the things that are Caesar's, and to God the things that are God's" (Mark 12:17b, Matthew 22:21b, Luke 20:25). An uncritical hearing or reading of these words leaves one quite satisfied. Of course, Jesus realized the dual loyalty of every citizen of that day, as we must of this day. There are certain responsibilities due the community, and there are specific ones due God. The problem appears when you ask the next question: Where do Caesar's rights over the individual's loyalty and life end and God's begin? That is not so easy to answer. Everyone admits his responsibility to maintain law and order, to supply education and aid in a community; but has the state the right to regiment a man's thoughts and actions, presumably for the good of the community? That question will remain unanswered for generations to come. One thing is perfectly sure, however, and that is that, for Jesus, God's Will is supreme and for another person or one's family or one's nation to forbid the free expression of that Will in human choice and obedience is sin and compromise (Matthew 10:37,38 and Luke 14:25,27).

Then there is Jesus' relation to women and children. Whether or not it was due to early female influences, one thing is certain: Luke's Gospel appears to record more instances than any other concerning Jesus' relationship to women. Perhaps the clearest expression of the Semitic attitude toward women is given in the fourth Gospel (4:1–42). The woman of Samaria stands aghast that Jesus should dare to speak to her, a woman, and a Samaritan woman at that. Yet that incident appears to be typical of Jesus'

The Faith He Lived 63

approach to womankind. In his eyes the differences were only biological; in the nature and attributes of their personalities there was no marked difference. On a later occasion Jesus stated a correlative idea, that in resurrection there would be neither male nor female, for all human souls are alike, children of God the Father (Mark 12:25, Matthew 22:30, and especially Luke 20:36). Therefore, in Jesus' eyes, women were always regarded as his kinswomen (Mark 3:31-35, Matthew 12:40-46, Luke 8:19-21). They were not to be discriminated against legally (cf. John 7:35—8:11) or maritally (Mark 10:6-9, Matthew 19:4-6, Luke 16:18). Jesus' concern for the widow of Nain (Luke 7:11-17), for the health of Jairus' daughter and the woman with the issue of blood (Mark 5:21-42, Matthew 9:18-26, Luke 8:40-56), for the redemption of the adulterous woman (John 4:1-42 or John 7:53—8:11) and for the companionship of Martha and Mary of Bethany (Luke 10:38-42), as well as that for his female disciples (Luke 8:1-3), shows Jesus' high regard for womanhood. This is the more startling when we note his failure to marry, and his apparent neglect of his mother from the beginning of his public ministry until the moment of his death (cf. Mark 3:31-35 with John 19:26-27).

Then there are children. Childhood in Jesus' day was a strenuous, haphazard and uncertain existence. Except in the rabbinic training of the boys, not much was provided for the wholesome development of the child. That development came despite circumstances, the Jews reasoning, evidently, that God had planned it so. Jesus, however, appears to be the first figure in history to recognize the child for its own sake. Gospel writers are unaware of their service to mankind at this point. They merely recorded what they had heard; yet in their accounts is imbedded the wondrous appreciation of children which Jesus evidently had. Just as Jesus was keenly aware of the situations of the lilies of the field, the foxes in their woods, the birds of the air, so he appeared to know the inner motivations, the external responses and the very thought of little children. He had watched them at play (Matthew 11:17, Luke 7:32); he had observed their humility (Matthew 18:2–4), and he portrayed them as God had created them (Mark 10:13–16, Matthew 19:13–15, Luke 18:15–17). For Jesus, true greatness was genuinely expressed in one's attitude toward children (Mark 9:33–37, Matthew 18:1–5, Luke 9:46–48). Real abundant living was exemplified in the life of the little child. Jesus saw with the Psalmist (8:2) that "out of the mouths of babes and sucklings have you perfected praise" (Matthew 21:16). For Jesus, childlike faith and spirit were intended by God for all mankind, whatever the chronological age, the sex, the race, the faith. As Jesus watched little children, he sought to recapture that childlike state of soul, and he found in it spiritual vigor and power. Then he sought to share this quality of faith with all whom he came in contact with. Jesus believed that except as one turns (repents) and becomes as a little child, he can in no wise enter the Kingdom of God (cf. Matthew 18:13).

In Regard to His Enemies

One cannot truthfully say that Jesus ever thought of his opponents as "enemies." Yet in the general parlance of the common people, that is what they were. Who were these "enemies" whom Jesus had to face, and in facing them revealed aspects of his faith? They were primarily from among five groups: the Pharisees, the scribes, the Sadducees, the Roman soldiers, and the unresponsive individuals. Their attitudes consisted of indifference, anger, disrespect and craftiness. Our interest, however, is in Jesus' response to these people whom he appears to antagonize.

The first recorded instance of antagonism to Jesus and his followers happened, according to Luke, on Jesus' final journey to Jerusalem (Luke 9:51–56). Jesus attempted to go directly from Galilee to Judea by way of Samaria. The Samaritans reacted, as was their custom, against Jewish pilgrims going to the Holy City, and refused Jesus and his friends hospitality. The sons of Zebedee demanded action in retaliation for the insult delivered their beloved master. But Jesus evidently realized the situation and, understanding the Samaritan attitude, rebuked his friends and moved on to what the Greek implies was "another kind" of town, presumably a Jewish settlement. His calm and poise revealed his understanding and sympathy in this tense situation.

Jesus' response to another annoying situation appears not to have been so calm. After an extended ministry in the great commercial centers of Galilee (Capernaum, Chorazin and Bethsaida), Jesus with a feeling of righteous indignation upbraided the inhabitants vigorously for their indifference and unresponsiveness. Sodom and Gomorrah would fare better than these cities, he cried. Those ruins in Jesus' day made people well aware of the sinfulness of bygone days of prosperity, but the Galilean towns were not aware of any such plight in store for them. Therefore Jesus felt called upon to shock them awake and to bring them to their senses (Matthew 11:20-24, Luke 10:13-15). Vigorous and apparently rebellious though he seemed to be, Jesus was inwardly poised and controlled. For a moment, his very being shook with the spirit of the ancient prophets of Israel. The wrath of God was striking a balance with the Love of God.

A similar feeling was expressed in the incident of Temple-cleansing (Mark 11:15-19, Matthew 21:12-17, Luke 19:45-48; cf. John 2:13-16). In placing the incident during the last week of Jesus' ministry, Mark, Matthew and Luke are undoubtedly more historically accurate than the fourth Gospel, which has placed it early in his public ministry. Although some have regarded Jesus' action in cleansing the Gentile court of all its merchandise as symbolic of his concern for the non-Jewish God-seekers, it would appear that Jesus was all for purging Judaism of its commercialism and materialism. Although some have used this passage as evidence of Jesus' approval of the use of force (in contrast to nonresistance), one must note that the cord (only mentioned in John 2:15) was used only on the animals. It would be fairer to the evidence if we acknowledge this seemingly violent action on Jesus' part to be an outburst of sincere feeling similar to his upbraiding of the Galilean cities (Matthew 11:20-24 and Luke

10:13–15) and of the Pharisees (Luke 11:42–44 and its parallels) and scribes (Luke 11:45–52 and its parallels): a parental prophetic call to repentance, to rethinking, and to redirection of life. During the whole melee Jesus appears to stand, in stark contrast to the moneychangers, calm and serene; he was certain within himself that he had acted upon God's behalf, not arbitrarily or despotically but with a high purpose and for the good of all concerned. This is the real motivation of abundant living: to lose one's self in order to really find one's self.

In a similar vein we could investigate Jesus' response to those accusers who contended he was in league with Beelzebub (Matthew 12:22–24, Luke 11:14–16), the sign-seekers (Matthew 12:38–40, Luke 11:29–30), the Pharisees (Luke 11:42–44 and parallels) and the scribes (Luke 11:45–52 and parallels). In dealing with his most intimate friends, likewise, he felt called upon to speak up sharply on such occasions as the instance when he called Peter Satan (Mark 8:33, Matthew 16:23). Yet underneath all this vigorous controversy we find Jesus the compassionate soul. Condemning the sins, he loved the sinners: "Father, forgive them; for they know not what they do" (Luke 23:34). These words he spoke on the cross, when he could have reviled against the murderers of innocent men. Perpetually patient, only occasionally perturbed, Jesus remained calm but resolute of soul. He had done his best; he could do no more: it was now in God's hands to complete the task. This is evidence of a stalwart faith in the righteousness of God.

In Regard to Himself

Innumerable books have been written on the subject of Jesus' sense of mission, known as "his messianic consciousness." It is not our purpose here to present a fresh study or to summarize their findings; rather, we hope to acknowledge those typical occasions when, not teaching, Jesus accepted or rejected certain aspects of his reputation.

The Faith He Lived

For instance, on one occasion a certain woman spoke boldly in flattering terms concerning him. Jesus rebuffed her by refusing to accept the pleasantry and by turning the crowd's attention to his beatitude: "Blessed rather are those who hear the word of God and keep it!" (Luke 11:28.)

On another day a certain man known as the rich young ruler came to him and in addressing Jesus said, "Good Master" (Mark 10:17–18, Matthew 19:17, Luke 18:18–19). Jesus' response is very enlightening and reveals his own inner sense of relationship to God: only God is good. If Jesus had accepted the enthusiastic acclaim of the young man he would not be manifesting his general spirit and nature. It would have manifested a streak of conceit in his nature, no matter how humbly he might try to bow out of the honor. Jesus recognized that to accept the honor of being declared or called "good" he would be acting insincerely, in a hypocritical manner. Therefore, true to his deepest nature, Jesus forestalled his answer to the young man's question by first correcting the appellation in order to set the record straight. His only desire in life was to be well-pleasing in God's sight, and to become perfect as his Heavenly Father was perfect.

This same sense of unworthiness in his own inner being is evident in the struggle in the garden of Gethsemane. We have already dealt with it in terms of his faithfulness to God's Will. Let us note here the disparity which is revealed in those fate-filled words between himself and God. "Not my will, but thine, be done" (Luke 22:42; cf. Mark 14:36, Matthew 26:39). Could it be that Jesus was actually admitting that his own will at that moment might or might not be in agreement with the Father's? Certainly these words reveal a strong loyalty to God. It reminds one of the words of Job: "Yea, though he slay me, yet will I trust him" (cf. Job 13:15).

Much has been written concerning the prayer life of Jesus, but hardly any of the writers have recognized in Jesus' praying the fact of his evident need for such spiritual renewal from time to time. Mark recalls that Jesus frequently withdrew early in the morning before others were awake (Mark 1:35), and often late in the evening after a strenuous day (cf. Mark 6:46). He recalls that it was usually a solitary place, and many times a mountain retreat. Jesus was praying when he came up out of the baptismal waters (Luke 3:21). He withdrew into the wilderness to pray, and there was tempted. He sought the desert place for prayer after the multitudes had been dispersed (Luke 5:16). He prayed when he was about to choose the Twelve (Luke 6:12) and just before he asked them what they thought of him (Luke 9:18). The Transfiguration took place during a period of prayer (Luke 9:28). He was arrested in Gethsemane after a period of prayer (Mark 14:32). And Luke records two prayers on the cross (Luke 23:34,46). The prayer life of Jesus so impressed the disciples that Luke recorded (11:1) that it was at the close of a prayer that the disciples asked the Master to teach them how to pray as he did, and he sketched out a pattern which we call the Lord's Prayer.

Several important facts should be noted in connection with this prayer life of the Master. First and foremost is the evident fact that Jesus felt the need to pray. Some Christological concepts, such as those which emphasize unduly his deity, do not include a praying Jesus. Those who hold such concepts are at a loss how to explain the overwhelming evidence in all four Gospels to this practice of Jesus. Nevertheless Jesus prayed; and he prayed because he felt the need to. He prayed at the great moments of crisis and decision. Turning points in his life were apparently first met in prayer, and upon the basis of new insight and of the Father's blessing he went forth resolute and unafraid. Furthermore, these prayer periods were seasons of refreshing and invigorating experience for Jesus. When he was tired, confused, and tense from dealing with crowds, Jesus found the tremendous release of prayer; he found that prayer re-created his whole being—body, mind and spirit.

Jesus appears to have had no sense of religious self-sufficiency and personal adequacy. His intuitive moral judgments and his consciousness of authority to proclaim God's Will came as the results of long hours spent in profound meditation and earnest

The Faith He Lived

prayer wherein he sought to ascertain the purposes of God. These were moments of Jesus' process of attuning to the spirit, mind and will of God. In prayer and meditation Jesus sensitized his whole being to the Will of God for his life.

A totally different type of action on Jesus' part likewise reflects his way of life. Early in his ministry Jesus was accosted by critics who had been comparing his actions with those of the ascetic Baptist. Why is it, they asked, that both of you preach the same message and claim to represent the same God, yet John lives the hermit life, "eating no bread and drinking no wine" (Luke 7:33), while you, Jesus, are noted for your social activities? He was reported to be "a glutton and a drunkard, a friend of tax collectors and sinners!" (Luke 7:34.) A very revealing comment! Jesus was evidently a very sociable person, one who enjoyed good times and good fellowship. The record is abundantly clear at this point. He attended weddings (John 2:1–12); he was the guest at banquets (Luke 7:36–50, and Luke 14:15 and Luke 11:37 and Mark 2:13–15, Matthew 9:10, Luke 4:29, and Luke 19:1–10, and Mark 14:3–9, Matthew 26:6–13; cf. John 12:1–8); he spoke often of such parties (Matthew 22:1–10, Luke 14:15–24, and Matthew 25:1–13), and on the last night in which he was betrayed he played host (Mark 14:22–26, Matthew 26:26–30, Luke 22:15–21, I Cor. 11:23–25; cf. John 6:35–48). One of the few details of the Golden Day in the future, when the ultimate in God's destiny for mankind would take place, was the expectation on Jesus' part of a great Messianic Feast (Mark 14:25, Matthew 16:29, Luke 22:18). That should be sufficient evidence to reveal that Jesus preferred a happy, joyous life to a cold, ascetic one. He believed that God intended human existence to be full, wholesome, exuberant and filled with many occasions for good fellowship about banquet tables. The more abundant life which Jesus sought to share was free and enjoyable. To his critics this was exercise of license, gluttonous, drunken and not at all the serious, sedate, ascetic life which was commonly thought of as worthy of being called religious, spiritual, godly. Yet Jesus did live in this more enthusiastic manner, and apparently expected his disciples to live in like manner (Mark 2:18–20, Matthew 9:14–15, Luke 5:33–35).

There is one final incident in Jesus' life that reveals a very significant estimate of himself. This is the so-called triumphal entry (Mark 11:1–11, Matthew 21:1–11, Luke 19:28–44, John 12:12–19). Truly, this was a dramatic act of prophetic character; something akin to the spiritual urge of the ancient prophets prompted him to present his message in a more spectacular manner than before. Peter's confession and the Transfiguration were positive proofs that his message had at last germinated in the souls of at least a few persons. Shown that it was possible for a few, he sought to stimulate the many. The essence of the idea is expressed by the writer of the fourth Gospel (12:32) when he has Jesus say, "And I, when I am lifted up from the earth, will draw all men to myself." Supposedly uttered by Jesus in anticipation of his crucifixion and elevation upon a wooden cross, these words were expressed here during the triumphal entry. The promise was realized on a later day, at Pentecost (Acts 4:31, 2:1–42). The very fact that Jesus planned and executed this daring and dangerous feat shows, however, one aspect of his self-esteem: although seriously aware of his own inner weaknesses, he was nevertheless conscious of his exceptional life, derived from God, a by-product of his intimate fellowship with the Father. Anticipating the words of the Apostle Paul, Jesus regarded himself somewhat the "first of many brethren" (Romans 8:29)—all sons of God, heirs together not only of the sufferings of this earth but also of the glories of eternal life (cf. Romans 8:17).

Thus we see Jesus refusing to be identified with the popular notions of messiahship. He believed that in a peculiar way he possessed knowledge of the steps to be taken toward the maturity of the human personality. These were what he called "the keys of the kingdom." These steps of human growth and development he felt called upon to share and expound. These "keys" he dramatically imparted to his intimate disciples, indicating there-

The Faith He Lived 71

by that they were to share them with each succeeding generation unto the ultimate redemption of all mankind (Matthew 16:19).

In Regard to His Participation in the Religious Practices of His Day

One further area of religious living remains to be investigated for the light it may throw upon our study of the faith of Jesus. This area pertains to Jesus' participation in, or abstention from, the religious practices of his day.

Luke's Gospel (4:16) appears to be the only one to declare that it was customary for Jesus to attend regularly various meetings of the synagogue. Further references to his synagogue attendance (Mark 3:1, Matthew 12:9, Luke 6:6, Matthew 14:23 and Matthew 9:35, Luke 13:10 and Mark 6:1,2, Matthew 13:35 and Mark 1:23, Luke 4:33 and Luke 4:44) attest to this Lucan comment. When his fame had spread, he rarely entered the synagogues in various towns and cities without being asked to speak. His messages, however, appear to have been out of the ordinary, and as tension grew he felt compelled to forsake the synagogue meetings. Afterwards he relied upon open-air services (Matthew 5:1, Mark 6:56; cf. Matthew 14:13–21 and parallels, Mark 7:31–8:10 and parallels; cf. John 16:2). Jesus found great value in these synagogue meetings, which were probably used, in that day, less for worship than for scribal interpretations of the Scriptures. From an early age Jesus reveled in such meetings (Luke 2:46,47). Stephen and Paul followed Jesus in this practice, and early missionaries of the Church also found the synagogue an excellent place to initiate their evangelistic effort for the faith.

Jesus likewise regarded the Temple of some value. It is significant to realize that even when Jesus felt compelled to cleanse the Temple, it was merely of its commercialism and materialism, not of its symbolism, ceremony and ritual. He allowed the expensive and seemingly useless sacrifices to continue. The evidence of his attendance at various feasts within holy confines (Feast of Booths, October, A.D. 29, John 7,8,9, cf. Luke 10:38 ff.; Feast of Dedication, December, A.D. 29, John 10, cf. Luke 17:11 ff.; Feast of Passover, John 2:23, 6:4, 11:55 and Mark 14:12, Matthew 26:17, Luke 22:7) reveals the respect Jesus had for its services of worship. Dare we admit to ourselves that he likewise purchased and sacrificed the various animals and cereals required by the Torah? We have no clear evidence that either he or his disciples actually did, but his very presence at the Temple at feast times and the absence of any contemporary criticism of his lack of participation appear to point to this startling conjecture as fact; undoubtedly Jesus was quite in agreement with the practices. It must be assumed, however, that he participated in a serious and worshipful spirit, and not in the manner of the hypocrites. Whether Jesus really felt as the great prophets did concerning sacrifices is unknown, but no one reading Micah 6:1–8 can escape the thought "How Christian!" Even though the early Christians continued to attend the Temple services out of habit (cf. Acts 3:1), the very fact that when the Temple was destroyed in A.D. 70, the mind and spirit of Jesus had so permeated the membership of the Church that no further attempt was made to maintain its spiritual values in some kind of substitute service. Sabbath-day observances were ultimately transferred to the Christians' "Lord's Day" services; but nothing really replaced the Temple services unless one would declare that the sacrificial interpretations placed upon the Last Supper or the commemorative services for the early martyrs were an attempt at some suitable substitute. Even though Jesus appeared to have supported the Temple by his attendance, participation and tribute, his teachings and probably the attitudes he expressed during the meetings pointed the way to the ultimate abolition of all sacrificial services in worship among his followers.

In regard to Jesus' use of the Sabbath there are several interesting aspects to note. First, it is quite obvious that Jesus customarily attended the synagogue or the Temple on the Sabbath day (cf. Luke 4:16). It is interesting to note that on those occasions when he took his disciples through the grainfields on the Sabbath (Mark 2:23–28, Matthew 12:1–6, Luke 6:1–5) he was not criticized for disobeying the two-thousand-cubit limit of Sabbath day walking nor for stealing someone's grain, but for "working," i.e., rubbing the kernels of wheat in the palms of his hands, regarded as thrashing and winnowing. Jesus, however, defended his actions by scriptural references to David (cf. I Samuel 21:1–6, Leviticus 24:9). Moreover, there appear to be several occasions when he healed individuals on the Sabbath—the man with the unclean spirit (Mark 1:23–27, Luke 4:31–35), the man with a withered hand (Mark 3:1–6, Luke 6:6–10, Matthew 12:9–13) and the hunch-backed woman (Luke 13:10), as well as others (Mark 1:32–34, cf. 8:16 and Luke 4:40). This is definitely a breaking of the Torah as the devout Pharisees interpreted it, but for Jesus it was only as much an exception as doing the farm chores or rescuing an unfortunate animal from its predicament (Matthew 12:11). Usually the day was given over to teaching (Luke 4:16 and Mark 1:21, Luke 4:31 and Mark 6:2–6 and Luke 13:10). In every instance of Sabbath use, Jesus expressed his faith: "The sabbath was made for man, not man for the sabbath" (Mark 2:27). And it is rather fascinating to realize that Jesus was hurriedly laid in Joseph's tomb just before the Sabbath began.

There remain two other minor incidents worthy of note in this connection. The first is the attitude of Jesus as expressed in his commands to the healed leper (Mark 1:44, Matthew 8:4, Luke 5:14). Jesus showed that he had great faith when he dared to touch the leper, for to do so was to make one's self at least "ceremonially unclean." But the point that is being made here is that despite Jesus' pronouncement of health he felt compelled (by social custom?) to command the leper to fulfill the ceremonial requirements for being approved as healed. These were not necessary, actually, since the man was healed. Jesus respects the sensitivity of others, however, and shows an unusual respect for ceremony in his command to the leper (cf. Luke 17:14). Another significant action on Jesus' part was his freedom in forgiving sin (cf. Mark 2:1–12, Matthew 9:1–8, Luke 5:17–26). In Jesus' day only priests could officially pronounce divine forgiveness of sin. In olden days prophets had also. By what line of reasoning Jesus felt free to do that which was forbidden we shall never know. It may have been that he regarded himself one of the line of prophets; it may have been because he did not believe that the exclusive rights should be in the hands of a select group, the priests. Or, most probably, it was due to the faith Jesus had in God: that as he had been endowed with the ability to heal, so he had been given the prerogative to pronounce divine forgiveness. In no instance does Jesus himself forgive sins; rather, what he did was to say those words which made it possible for the sinner to surmount his fears and sense of guilt, and take advantage of the forgiveness of God.

Summary

We have endeavored to indicate some of the aspects of that faith which made possible a life unequaled in human history. This is the life of faith as Jesus lived it, and as he sought to impart it to other men. It was childlike in its simplicity, humility, respectfulness and enthusiasm, yet virile, strong, courageous and life-giving all at the same time.

Real religion involves the whole of life. In this section we have studied to some degree the social ethics of Jesus—not as he taught it, but as he lived it. We have watched his response to the needs of humanity on every hand; the outcast publican and sinner, the socially undesirable handicapped person—the foreigner, the political dictator, the religious hierarchy, and benighted womanhood and childhood. Upon each group he placed a blessing that has resounded down through the centuries to result in what we call concern for the common man. Each group has increasingly received the benefits of that blessing as each succeeding generation of his disciples has lived that life anew. Only where each individual lives the life of Jesus in his own generation will ultimate peace and good will come among men.

CHAPTER V

THE FAITH HE EXPECTED

The faith of Jesus can next be seen in the set of requirements which the records claim Jesus expected of his disciples. We are convinced by the evidence available that what Jesus required of his intimate disciples had first been required of him, and had been found satisfying and rewarding.

The less familiar invitation to discipleship given by Jesus is found only in Matthew's Gospel (11:28–30):

> (1) Come to me, all who labor and are heavy-laden, and I will give you rest. Take my yoke upon you, and learn from me; for I am gentle and lowly in heart, and you will find rest for your souls. For my yoke is easy, and my burden is light.

It has been widely suggested that this saying is merely a quotation from some Jewish book of wisdom that has been placed in the mouth of Jesus either by Matthew or his sources. Others suggest that Jesus himself made the selection. But close scrutiny shows that neither interpretation is necessary. Rather, we have here a genuine saying of Jesus. The key word is the "my" just before the word "yoke." Jewish wisdom literature often speaks of the Torah as "a yoke," but the pronoun here indicates that Jesus was not speaking of the yoke of the Torah, but rather the yoke of the Kingdom. Therefore, for one to accept the invitation of Jesus and take upon himself the yoke of the Kingdom was to acknowledge the sovereignty of God and to give himself to God's service. It is interesting to note that Jesus expected this to be accomplished by learning from him. This learning was not merely to be the reception of instructions, but to be participation in the exemplary life-pattern of Jesus himself. Jesus claimed that the way was easy and light in comparison to the yoke of the Torah. Where the Torah weighted men down with the heavy burdens of minute details, the Kingdom gave relief to the weary and heavy-laden. Interpretatively translated, this invitation would read: "Become my disciples, all ye who are weary and heavy-laden with the requirements of the Torah and the problems of this life, for I promise relief for your hearts and minds. Accept the yoke of the Kingdom and learn from me what I have learned, for I would share this way of life with you. Then you will receive the blessings and fulfillment of your lives. Then you will live at peace with all men in the Kingdom of God. This kingdom-way is easy and joyously abundant. Enter thou the Kingdom of God."

Here we have an exceptionally vivid statement concerning Jesus' whole thought of his ministry and message. He believed that he had been chosen by God for an itinerant ministry at the moment of his baptism at the hands of John. His wilderness sojourn had been more than a time of temptation; it was also a time for searching out the aim and message of his ministry. What was he supposed to share with people? How was he to impart it to them? Here in this Matthean passage (11:28–30) we have a clear pronouncement of his message. He was to proclaim this new way of life, which had brought such satisfaction (salvation) to him; he was sure that it would do the same for others. He believed that it was the very revealed word and will of God. Ultimately he came to realize how unique he was in this regard, and began to think of himself as God's Messiah. He saw that his mission was to be the gathering together of like-minded God-inspired people who shared with him the abundant life of the spirit.

The more familiar invitation to discipleship is found in Mark's Gospel, the prime recorder. The theme with which Jesus began his ministry was this:

(2) The time is fulfilled, and the kingdom of God is at hand; repent, and believe in the gospel. (Mark 1:15)

This statement is quite clear-cut in its pronouncement, but difficulties arise as soon as one attempts to interpret its meaning. This is due chiefly to the apparent variety of interpretations placed upon it by the Jews, the early disciples and the Gospel writer of a later date. Our concern is primarily with the connotations Jesus placed upon the various words and phrases, irrespective of that of his hearers.

What did Jesus mean when he said, "The time is fulfilled"? Undoubtedly he meant to imply that with the opening of his public ministry he personally had come to feel that a new age was dawning. Whether or not he would agree with his hearers that this meant that the Messianic Age was about to burst in upon them is still a moot question. It is now generally accepted by a great many scholars that Jesus did not expect, as did his more anxious hearers, a great heavenly cataclysm, preceded by many terrifying experiences on earth and crowned with the visible appearance of the Deity in power and great glory. Such an apocalyptic concept of the coming of the Kingdom of God was strictly Jewish and strongly nationalistic. Jesus appears to have believed that the Kingdom of God was primarily the reign of God in the wills and souls of men. Therefore, when he proclaimed, "The time is fulfilled," he was calling the attention of people of every race to his message, which he regarded as fresh, new, life-changing and completely satisfying.

"The kingdom of God is at hand." All of Jesus' ministry and teachings appear to counter any idea that he was a thoroughgoing apocalyptist, as many of his followers were. When Jesus proclaimed the Kingdom to be "at hand," he was seeking to state unequivocally that the Kingdom was here, as it always had been, but that men had not become aware of its presence. They had been led astray by their blind leaders (Matthew 23:16, 15:14). Their leaders had proclaimed only its future culmination; they failed to indicate its present reality in the lives of men. Now Jesus proposed to reveal this fact not only by his daily living but by his public pronouncements. He believed that God had "called" him for this specific purpose.

"Repent ye!" Did Jesus mean by this phrase that the first step in preparation to enter this new life of the Kingdom was a remorseful and almost morbid sense of sorrow for past sins? That is what traditional Christianity has always maintained in their interpretation of the Gospel. The Greek word used in this instance in the text is *metanoia*, and this primarily means exactly what the English word, from the French, implies—"rethink ye," "change your mind," "accept a new outlook on life," "remold your way of life according to a new point of view" (i.e., repent ye!). Thus we see that, if the records are correctly reporting Jesus, he was applying a more healthy-minded approach to salvation than has been commonly accepted in the Church. It reminds one of Paul's vivid saying, ". . . forgetting what lies behind and straining forward to what lies ahead, I press on toward the goal for the prize of the upward call of God" (Phil. 3:13*b*-14*ab*). In this approach Jesus was expressing the secret of his life-equality. As "I have overcome the world" (John 16:33*c*), so may ye!

"And believe in the gospel." Here we see Jesus' emphasis upon faith. It was not enough to believe that a new age was about to dawn, nor was it sufficient to repent. Having caught the vision, the new outlook upon life which Jesus shares from his own experience, one then must have faith to launch out and live in accordance with these new attitudes, guiding principles and moral and spiritual insights. One never really "believes" until one "acts on faith" in keeping with the new idea, the new concept, the new pattern of life. The Kingdom of God comes only when individual human beings accept and live by the Will of God, "as though the kingdom was already here." When individuals live in this way, they participate in the new life; they enter the reality of the Kingdom of God. The Kingdom of God

The Faith He Expected

is here not only in their inward parts but also in their social activities.

Such a message as this was profoundly original with Jesus. It appears to have been so much like and yet so different from contemporary, popular concepts that for the most part the people lacked deeper insights into its content and reality. Even his intimate disciples failed miserably at this very point, despite their rather frequent flashes of insight into what the Master was saying and doing. Scrap the old concepts; lay hold upon the new, and the Divine Truth which underlies both will spring alive into a newness of life that will astound mankind. Herein Jesus filled old terms with new meanings and allowed them to reveal the truth of God he so much desired to share.

This was the very experience of Jesus himself, from the moment in his childhood when he began asking questions to his dying day. Jesus' alert mind was ever testing new ideas as well as old. It is worthy of note that the story of his *bar mizvah* trip to Jerusalem at the age of twelve centered around the fact that he was found discussing issues with the doctors of the Torah. Repentance therefore was a matter of rethinking for Jesus. He had once accepted the rabbinic and popular concepts of religion and of theology; once he had not given much thought to the task of the moneychangers in the Temple. His adolescent mind and sensitive soul had changed all that. He had questioned the many practices of his people. He had argued over the points of the Law with the rabbis, scribes and doctors. He had taken every opportunity to think and meditate; and his manual occupation gave him such time to think. His wilderness sojourn after his baptism demonstrates this inclination of his being. Such intellectual and spiritual questing made for life-changing experiences and the development of his person. The changed mind supplemented by the changed will was the key to the more abundant life which now he sought to impart to others. To experience that unfolding life was to attain personal maturity and to participate in communal living through wholesome relationships.

Thus Jesus came to speak of the Kingdom in rather contradictory terms: it was here yet it was to come; it was present but its fulfillment was in the future; it was invisible yet it was always visible; it was of heavenly origin, but it was for earthly living. The important point for the individual was to launch out in faith upon this new way of life. Then, and then alone, would God's Will act in individual lives and in the social group. Man would experience eternal life, and society would culminate in the Kingdom of God.

The invitation given, disciples appeared. Evidently there were two types of disciples: those chosen by Jesus, and those who themselves chose to become his disciples. Regarding the former we know the following facts. First, Jesus personally chose five: Peter, Andrew, James, John and Matthew. The records (Mark 1:16,20, 2:13–17 and parallels) give no evidence of requirements demanded or accepted. We do learn later, however, that Peter felt the discipline rather trying at times (Mark 10:28, Matthew 19:27, Luke 18:28). "Lo, we have left everything and followed you. What then shall we have?" (Matthew 19:27.) The standards whereby Jesus chose the remaining seven Apostles from among a larger group of intimate disciples have been lost to posterity, if they ever were known. The records (Mark 3:16–19, Matthew 10:2–4, Luke 6:14–16, Acts 1:13) merely reveal that a special occasion was observed for the official and public establishment of the Twelve and simply record the names of the men chosen (and even in that regard there are some minor variations). The remaining eleven upon the death of Judas Iscariot felt led to replace him, and it is interesting to note the qualifications they set up (Acts 1:21–22). They do not appear to have selected him on the basis of spirituality or moral integrity. Rather, the account intimates that the choice was based on whether or not he had shared in a resurrection appearance (Acts 1:22*b*), and whether or not he was one of the earliest followers of Jesus (Acts 1:21–22*a*). These two qualifications are interesting in that they imply that there were disciples who could fulfill one but very few who could qualify in both. The fact is that only two of those present in Jerusalem at that strategic moment could so qualify (Acts 1:23).

Some of the remaining "unchosen" disciples probably felt that Jesus had been rather arbitrary in his selecting process, if not showing some favoritism. Their love for him, however, undoubtedly overcame any jealous feelings.

When we turn to those few selected passages (Matthew 8:19–22, Luke 9:57–62) recording the pleas of those who desired discipleship, we learn much of the standards which Jesus most likely expected of himself and certainly of the Twelve. In fact, we gain the impression that every disciple in every generation was expected to fulfill these requirements as a part of the discipline. Let us look at these incidents and cases:

(3) As they were going along the road, a man said to him, "I will follow you wherever you go." And Jesus said to him, "Foxes have holes, and birds of the air have nests; but the Son of man has nowhere to lay his head." To another he said, "Follow me." But he said, "Lord, let me first go and bury my father." But he said to him, "Leave the dead to bury their own dead; but as for you, go and proclaim the kingdom of God." Another said, "I will follow you, Lord; but let me first say farewell to those at my home." Jesus said to him, "No one who puts his hand to the plow and looks back is fit for the kingdom of God." (Luke 9:57–62; cf. Matthew 8:19–22)

This passage and its Matthean counterpart come from the collection of Jesus' sayings which was assembled very early by the Church and which is known to scholars as the written source Q. The Lucan form of the passage is generally preferred. Our interest, however, is not in the details of its *Sitz im Leben* but in the demands of Jesus. In the first instance Jesus attempts to make the would-be disciple consider the cost of discipleship. To follow Jesus in that day meant to do so physically as well as morally, intellectually and spiritually. Although Jesus pointed to the physical rigors demanded, he undoubtedly expected the candidates to include the moral, intellectual and spiritual rigors as well. In the second instance, Jesus said, in essence: Let that detail take care of itself: you (the candidate) have more important responsibilities to assume. Only Luke (9:60*b*) intimates what these were: go—preach, proclaim the imminence of the Kingdom, bear witness to the new life of the spirit which has awakened within you. Luke alone gives a third instance. Jesus appears to regard his mission as most urgent—so much so that there is no time for even a fond adieu for those most intimate.

In all three occurrences we have Jesus' attitude toward the cost and discipline of true discipleship, and we are convinced that it reflects his own sense of discipline and discipleship to the Father. What the Father demands and expects from him, he can no less require and expect from his disciples. He was merely giving voice to the Will of God in the matter: for others as much as for himself. Those who would be children of God, and in so doing become his followers and co-heirs of the Kingdom, must first of all count the cost of such allegiance. They must estimate the hardship to be endured if they are to keep their personal integrity in the matter. They must be willing to sacrifice their own desire and feeling. They must give absolute priority to the work of the Kingdom and to the way of life involved. And they must, finally, develop a singleness of purpose that is almost perfection itself.

Clearly this is the strict way of life that Jesus himself was living. At baptism he took the step to absolute obedience and singleness of purpose. He felt called upon to sacrifice his own desires for food, raiment and shelter as well as for family relationships and responsibilities. The demand of his mission he found extremely exacting. We, of course, know that it ultimately demanded his physical life as well, on the cross, but at this moment Jesus probably was not aware of this. He had already experienced, however, the hardship and cost as well as the thrill and joy of the new life he had found in and with God. Yet his continued faithfulness to the Father brought rich experiences of life; and this was Kingdom-living. So overflowing was this way of life that he sought to share it with all others, that in like manner each disciple might come into the same joy of salvation.

(4) And they were exceedingly astonished, and said to him, "Then who can be saved?" Jesus looked at them and said, "With men it is impossible, but not with God; for all things are possible with God." Peter began to say to him, "Lo, we have left everything and followed you." Jesus said, "Truly, I say to you, there is no one who has left house or brothers or sisters or mother or father or children or lands, for my sake and for the gospel, who will not receive a hundredfold now in this time, houses and brothers and sisters and mothers and children and lands, with persecutions, and in the age to come eternal life. But many that are first will be last, and the last first." (Mark 10:26–31; consult Matthew 19:25–30 and Luke 8:26–30)

Those who listened to Jesus' words asked, "Who, then, can be saved?" Parenthetically, it is interesting to note the use of "can" rather than "may." The listeners evidently believed more in the human ability to alert their spiritual sensitiveness to God's rejuvenating power than in the helplessness of men to do anything about their own salvation. The records appear to bear this truth out: man can and does do something in his own strength toward making himself receptive to the grace of God.

Let us return, however, to the listeners' question: "Who, then, can be saved?" Jesus' answer implied that it all depended upon God. Yet Jesus also said, "There is no one who has left house or brothers or sisters or mother or father or children or lands, for my sake and for the gospel, who will not receive a hundredfold now in this time . . ." (Mark 10:29–30*a*). Here we see God's action matched by man's. Jesus believed that absolute loyalty to God and His Kingdom would release one from the burdens of this world. He found it so in his own experience.

Therefore, those who are to be saved are they who both completely rely upon God's grace and earnestly step out in faith to possess the new life.

> (5) He who loves father or mother more than me is not worthy of me; and he who loves son or daughter more than me is not worthy of me; and he who does not take his cross and follow me is not worthy of me. (Matthew 10:37–38)
>
> Now great multitudes accompanied him; and he turned and said to them, "If any one comes to me and does not hate his own father and mother and wife and children and brothers and sisters, yes, and even his own life, he cannot be my disciple." (Luke 14:25–26)

These passages present one of the most uncompromising statements of the claims of the Kingdom. Here we see Jesus' own self-discipline reflected in what he believed was demanded by God of all who would share in this new life. Aligning one's self with the Kingdom, as he had done, meant taking a risk in regard to family relationships and to community responsibilities. He who accepted these risks with his eyes open was prepared, as Jesus apparently was, to accept all consequences that might ensue. Such total allegiance called for personal integrity, dogged endurance and continued enthusiasm throughout life. Jesus felt led to follow this path in his own life, and the results were so overwhelmingly satisfying that he could not expect anything less from those who sought to participate in this new and abundant life. Jesus found that the essence of the new way of life was not to be found in self-renunciation, nor in self-realization, but in self-consecration to the Will of God.

There are two other occasions during Jesus' ministry which strike a similar note. On one of these Jesus said: "No one can serve two masters; for either he will hate the one and love the other, or he will be devoted to the one and despise the other. You cannot serve God and mammon." (Matthew 6:24; cf. Luke 16:13.) Did Jesus learn this lesson from hard experience? If it was not his own experience, he was a keen observer of other men's predicaments. Total consecration is the key.

On the other occasion, the sons of Zebedee were pleading for the seats of honor in the coming Kingdom, and Jesus replied, "You do not know what you are asking. Are you able to drink the cup that I drink, or to be baptized with the baptism with which I am baptized?" (Mark 10:38.) Here Jesus was indicating something of the cost of true discipleship. He expected them to share in the disciplines expected of him.

Undoubtedly these passages were remembered by the early church, because they were found pertinent to the life-decisions of the members in later hours of persecution. Taken at face value, they are harsh words. One wonders just what motivated Jesus to put them in just these forms in the first place. It is doubtful that the persecutions he had endured thus far in his ministry would have caused him to express such drastic words of warning. Probably Jesus saw more clearly than they the incompatibility of the new way of life with that accepted by society. Thus he was led to forewarn his followers of the probable cost, and to give them some inkling of the proper conduct during such periods of persecution.

> (6) I tell you, my friends, do not fear those who kill the body, and after that have no more that they can do. But I will warn you whom to fear: fear him who, after he has killed, has power to cast into hell; yes, I tell you, fear him! Are not five sparrows sold for two pennies? And not one of them is forgotten before God. Why, even the hairs of your head are all numbered. Fear not; you are of more value than many sparrows. (Luke 12:4–7; cf. Matthew 10:28–31)

A primary quality of a son of God is fearlessness. Who can be afraid when one puts one's whole faith in God, the Father and the Creator? One need not fear the bully, the persecutor or the dictator who may have power and ability to slaughter the body. It is God alone whom one should fear; for He has the power to kill not only the body but the soul as well. He may even cast the soul into hell. Jesus does not instigate fear alone in his warning; he balances his warning with a challenge to trust God. God is concerned not only with the birds of the air but with the hairs of the human head (Matthew 10:30). One may stand trembling before God the Judge, yet confidently before God the King, whose son and servant one is. In other words, Jesus was saying that no human persecution was to be allowed to corrupt the loyalty of his disciples, or to lessen their trust in God. It brings to mind the words of the Apostle Paul on this subject:

> Who shall separate us from the love of Christ? Shall tribulation, or distress, or persecution, or famine, or nakedness, or peril, or sword? . . . No, in all these things we are more than conquerors through him who loved us. For I am sure that neither death, nor life, nor angels, nor principalities, nor things present, nor things to come, nor powers, nor height, nor depth, nor anything else in all creation, will be able to separate us from the love of God in Christ Jesus our Lord. (Romans 8:35,37–39)

Such dogged loyalty is characteristic of Jesus' personal life, just as it became so for Paul's. Jesus is simply sharing a faith and a discipline which he has tested and found ennobling. As we have already recognized in the record concerning Jesus' prayer in Gethsemane (Mark 14:36, Matthew 26:39*b*, Luke 22:42), Jesus knew and paid the price for such faith: "Not my will, but thine, be done" (Luke 22:42*b*).

(7) And I tell you, every one who acknowledges me before men, the Son of man also will acknowledge before the angels of God; but he who denies me before men will be denied before the angels of God. And every one who speaks a word against the Son of man will be forgiven; but he who blasphemes against the Holy Spirit will not be forgiven. And when they bring you before the synagogues and the rulers and the authorities, do not be anxious how or what you are

to answer or what you are to say; for the Holy Spirit will teach you in that very hour what you ought to say. (Luke 12:8-12; cf. Matthew 10:32,33 and 12:32)

In time of persecution, one is advised to have utter faith in God, to abandon his fate to the Will of God. But should God seem far away in such a moment and the way gets hard, then put your loyalty in Jesus himself. For as one remains faithful to him and his way of life, one is actually manifesting one's loyalty and faith in God. In such a time of persecution the true sons of God will exercise faith, faith *with* God. Their source of courage and life is found in God. To Him they must remain steadfast. He will see them through, though their bodies be destroyed. He will inspire them with appropriate answers and words of testimony.

(8) And he [Jesus] said to his disciples, "Therefore I tell you, do not be anxious about your life, what you shall eat, nor about your body, what you shall put on. For life is more than food, and the body more than clothing. Consider the ravens: they neither sow nor reap, they have neither storehouse nor barn, and yet God feeds them. Of how much more value are you than the birds! And which of you by being anxious can add a cubit to his span of life? If then you are not able to do as small a thing as that, why are you anxious about the rest? Consider the lilies, how they grow; they neither toil nor spin; yet I tell you, even Solomon in all his glory was not arrayed like one of these. But if God so clothes the grass which is alive in the field today and tomorrow is thrown into the oven, how much more will he clothe you, O men of little faith? And do not seek what you are to eat and what you are to drink, nor be of anxious mind. For all the nations of the world seek these things; and your Father knows that you need them. Instead, seek his kingdom, and these things shall be yours as well. (Luke 12:22-31; cf. Matthew 6:25-33)

One of the most menacing hindrances to singleness of heart toward God is anxiety (or that which we more popularly call worry). The disciple is in danger of having business of his own to which he must attend before he can give himself unstintingly to God's work. This would undermine his trust in God.

Mankind down through the centuries has been more or less concerned with the necessities of life—food, raiment and shelter. These have inevitably absorbed a large proportion of man's thought and care. Now, Jesus is not despising or rejecting these fundamental necessities of life; rather, he is seeking to put them in their proper and relative place of importance in human experience. He warns against concentrating all one's interest and efforts upon such things. This reveals two things closely connected in Jesus' life: his appreciation and knowledge of God, and his faith in the providence of God.

Since God is the Heavenly Father, Jesus could not conceive of God's letting the child whom He loved starve while He fed others whose claim on Him was weaker, e.g., the birds and the plants. Here we see the character of God as Jesus perceived it: as Creator and Ruler of the universe and the natural order. While this is true, God's method is to proceed along uniform lines, i.e., what we have come to call "the laws of nature." Jesus pointed out, however, that God is intimately and deeply concerned with every detail of His creation and creative process.

Although it can be said that God exercises fatherly care for the birds and the lilies, yet it must be pointed out that God is not conceived by Jesus to be the Father of the birds and lilies. Rather, He is Father only to those beings who can realize Him as such, and whom He recognizes as sons. Jesus would have us see, also, that the Father's supreme passion is for Life. If he lavishes his gifts of food and raiment and shelter upon creations which can respond only with beauty and song, it is but reasonable to suppose that He will do no less upon those creatures who can reply with love and appreciation, if they but will to do so. The Providence which watches over the birds and the

The Faith He Expected

flowers can be trusted to protect and care for the disciples, who, in turn, in the face of desperation were expected to face up to persecution, hunger and death.

Once again words addressed to his disciples have revealed features of Jesus' personal faith. He was not preaching asceticism, nor did he place any religious value in starvation or nakedness. What he expected was faith in God and His providence, a sense of proportion or relativity, and a true evaluation of things. What Jesus is doing here is establishing a set of values to be the guiding principle for thought as well as for action. At the top stands the Will of God; nothing else can be understood or valued correctly until this is given priority. Once this has been done, the individual gains poise and confidence in the face of all danger, fear and anxiety. "Fear not, little flock, for it is your Father's good pleasure to give you the kingdom" (Luke 12:32).

> (9) Sell your possessions, and give alms; provide yourself with purses that do not grow old, with a treasure in the heavens that does not fail, where no thief approaches and no moth destroys. For where your treasure is, there will your heart be also. (Luke 12:33–34)

Here we have another recorded injunction which Jesus gave his disciples in preparation for days of persecution. The fact that the early church attempted to practice this precept (Acts 2:44–45, 4:32–37) appears to offer strong evidence for the authenticity of this saying. The saying represents the age-old idea that wealth is power; Jesus therefore appears to be expressing his faith in God rather than in mammon. Material things should serve man, not enslave him; for when they become his master, then the love, thought and service which man should devote to God and His Kingdom are put in second place, soon neglected and forgotten.

In conclusion to our study of Jesus' requirements for discipleship and warnings which he gave the disciples, we must note his instructions to them as they went forth on a special preaching mission:

> (10) Then he said to his disciples, "The harvest is plentiful, but the laborers are few; pray therefore the Lord of the harvest to send out laborers into his harvests." (Matthew 9:37; cf. Luke 10:2)
>
> Behold, I send you out as sheep in the midst of wolves; so be wise as serpents and innocent as doves. (Matthew 10:16; cf. Luke 10:3)

We notice Jesus' sense of urgency regarding his task. He has very little time for selfish pleasures himself; he does not expect any more for his disciples. His expectations here are not only his but God's upon him as well. These verses indicate that Jesus believed that God, the Lord of the harvest, was He who sent out the laborers into the fields. Jesus wished no credit for the undertaking; they were all undertaking it for God. We also note that Jesus regarded general society as "wolves"; in their customary selfishness men appeared as wolves in their cunning and recklessness toward one another and in their quest for material goods.

> Whenever you enter a town and they receive you, eat what is set before you; heal the sick in it and say to them, "The kingdom of God has come near to you." But whenever you enter a town and they do not receive you, go into its streets and say, "Even the dust of your town that clings to our feet, we wipe off against you; nevertheless know this, that the kingdom of God has come near." I tell you, it shall be more tolerable on that day for Sodom than for that town. (Luke 10:8–12; cf. Matthew 10:15)

This lays down the missionary methods employed by the disciples whom Jesus himself sent forth. The instructions fall into two groups: the procedure when the reception is friendly, and the procedure when the reception is hostile. In regard to the former, Jesus suggests that they accept the hospitality offered in the

The Faith He Expected

spirit in which it is offered. Here we have a typical expression of Jesus' faith in humanity and of his desire to serve those who are receptive. Jesus recommends that in instances of hostility they waste no time in expressing their displeasure. After a prophetic act of renunciation has been publicly performed as an exhortation and warning of the coming divine retribution, the disciples are to hurry on to the next town, for Jesus believed the time was short.

CHAPTER VI

THE FAITH HE SHARED

The final source of information concerning the various aspects of the faith of Jesus is a study of his teachings. What Jesus imparted as general instructions to others was consciously the sharing of his own faith and of the lessons learned through living it out in practice. Briefly stated, Jesus believed that the world in which we find ourselves has meaning which can be expressed in terms of the wise and all-pervading purpose of God. He believed that man's sin and misery can be explained in terms of man's ignorance, immaturity and deliberate opposition to that divine purpose. He believed that man has within his own nature all the potentialities of the divine image. He believed that man can fulfill the divine intent of his nature by means of utter submission of his will to God's. He believed that through filial piety and constant fellowship with the heavenly Father-God, man's life, both personal and social, acquires new quality, new integrity, new meaning, new direction and new hope. He believed that death was, like birth, only a passing phase in the developing and unfolding process of man's maturation. This faith, by which he lived and experienced the *joie de vivre,* he sought to impart to others. He did this not that his followers should slavishly imitate him, but that they might learn from him the secret of mature living.

The teachings of Jesus in their inmost nature are, therefore, bound up with his faith. For this reason they cannot be regarded as rules and regulations for human conduct. In fact, Jesus appears to have had only two rules or commandments for life: love of God, and love of neighbor (Mark 12:28–34 and parallels). Therefore his teachings must be approached from a slightly different point of view. They should be regarded as norms, at best as guides, for determining the degree of spiritual quality and righteousness within the individual or society. It is from this point of view that we shall approach the study of his teachings.

We shall present the selected passages from the teachings of Jesus in the order of the sources from which they have been taken: e.g., Q (written about A.D. 50), L (*ca.* A.D. 60), M (*ca.* A.D. 65), and "Mark" (*ca.* A.D. 70). Each selected passage will serve as a symbol for a certain aspect of Jesus' faith. Whenever there are other familiar sayings that coincide with the thought and faith expressed in the example, reference will be made to them.

From Q

(1) Seeing the crowds, he went up on the mountain, and when he sat down his disciples came to him. And he opened his mouth and taught them, saying:

"Blessed are the poor in spirit, for theirs is the kingdom of heaven.

"Blessed are those who mourn, for they shall be comforted.

"Blessed are the meek, for they shall inherit the earth.

"Blessed are those who hunger and thirst for righteousness, for they shall be satisfied.

"Blessed are the merciful, for they shall obtain mercy.

"Blessed are the pure in heart, for they shall see God.

"Blessed are the peacemakers, for they shall be called sons of God.

"Blessed are those who are persecuted for righteousness' sake, for theirs is the kingdom of heaven.

"Blessed are you when men revile you and persecute you and utter all kinds of evil against you falsely on my account. Rejoice and be glad, for your reward is great in heaven, for so men persecuted the prophets who were before you." (Matthew 5:1-12; cf. Luke 6:20-26)

This is a selected grouping of pithy sayings by Jesus. Everyone knows them as "The Beatitudes," yet they were not originally all uttered at once, as Luke's recording of them indicates. Each beatitude had its own *Sitz im Leben* which brought it forth from the mind and heart of Jesus. Each has a quality which reveals further aspects of Jesus' faith.

(i) In the first beatitude, "Blessed are the poor in spirit," we discover Jesus' appraisal of the effect of a rather discredited cause. The "poor in spirit," from the Pharisees' point of view, refers to the *am-ha-aretz,* or the peasants, of Palestine. They are referred to elsewhere in the Gospels as "the sinners," unworthy of the spiritual inheritance of Israel (reserved for the Pharisees, of course). Jesus pointed out, however, that this inheritance, a divine quality of life, is the by-product of a life-approach characterized by such words as "humility" and "teachableness." What Jesus said was, "Fortunate is the person who has this quality of life, for he will participate in God's fellowship and destiny. Only this quality of life is worthy of participating in the divine Kingdom."

(ii) The second beatitude, the circumstances for uttering which have been lost, is this: "Blessed are they who mourn, for they shall be comforted." In this saying Jesus shared his response to one of Life's most tense moments. Mourning is man's response to a deep, and sometimes terrifying, sense of loss. This loss may be occasioned by the physical death of a loved one; it may be occasioned by theft of a very precious possession. The loss leaves one weak, and ofttimes insecure. At this very moment of weakness God offers help. We forget the true meaning of comfort. We often mean by the word, or act, a sentimental utterance or a romantic gesture. "Comfort" comes, however, from two Latin words *cum* and *forte,* which mean "with strength." Therefore, if the translation is accurate, Jesus was not speaking lightly of this intensely personal experience. He proclaimed that when a man in his utter weakness turned to God he would receive strength to overcome his trial. Jesus heralded this truth because, first, he had experienced it in his own exercise of faith.

(iii) "Blessed are the meek, for they shall inherit the earth." Meekness for Jesus is in no wise spinelessness. As he stood his ground before the onslaught of his critics, as he remained stalwartly silent before the powerful Roman procurator, Jesus exemplified this beatitude. That man is meek who knows in whom he places his absolute trust and confidence and then proceeds with resolute courage to be as wise as a serpent and as innocent as a dove (cf. Matthew 10:16). Persons who wisely handle their lives when in positions of responsibility are the only ones worthy of directing the world's work for the improvement and fulfillment of humanity's potentialities and needs. The quality of meekness is one of the most important characteristics of mature man (redeemed man).

(iv) "Blessed are those who hunger and thirst for righteousness, for they shall be satisfied." The meaning of this beatitude is so clear that it almost beggars an explanation. It reveals, however, an item of faith in Jesus' appraisal of life. He is certain that those whose first concern in life is righteousness shall find and possess it. Of that Jesus has no doubt.

(v) "Blessed are the merciful, for they shall obtain mercy." In stating this truism, Jesus is in no sense implying that God's gift of mercy is as a reward for merciful acts performed by the individual, whether conscious or unaware of such a reward. Rather, he is intimating his belief that only when the individual participates in an experience of the eternal does one actually "receive" and "share" in the gifts of God. This is true not only in the area of mercy but in the areas of forgiveness, love and faith. This we shall see also in taking cognizance of the implications contained in the phrase of the Lord's Prayer which says, "Forgive us our debts, *as we* forgive our debtors." The emphasis has been consciously placed upon the two words "as we," for only "as we" enter into the exacting and loving activities of God shall we receive His blessings, however undeserving we may feel toward the whole situation. This is a significant aspect of Jesus' faith and the attitudes which he holds in connection with that faith.

(vi) "Blessed are the pure in heart, for they shall see God." Most interpreters take this verse in its literal sense, especially in connection with the phrase "the pure in heart." One must not overlook the fact, however, that the heart in the Semitic world was the seat of wisdom. Therefore, one must reinterpret the beatitude so that Jesus' original connotation may be seen. What Jesus said was this: "Fortunate are the wholesome-minded people, for they shall see God because they will be seeing *with* God." We have here an appeal to have the mind of God, to look upon life and its ultimate relationships from a divine vantage point and with a divine wisdom. We may gather from the passage that Jesus was indicating the condition upon which fellowship with God is possible; i.e., a pure heart motivates one to action worthy of a son of the Father. But even in such an understanding of the beatitude there is implied the much more subtle intimation of Jesus that such divine communion is based on nothing less than a unity of outlook and criteria of judgment for action. No doubt it is in this vein that the Johannine writer is thinking when he has Jesus say, "I and the Father are one" (John 10:30).

(vii) "Blessed are the peacemakers, for they shall be called sons of God." The first important point of this beatitude is found in the wise choice of the word "peacemaker." One should note that it does not read "peace-keeper," and for this we should be eternally grateful to Jesus for his semantic gift. Only peacemakers are worthy of being sons of God. God Himself is never a peace-keeper; He is eternally a peacemaker. Only he who has the ability to resolve the clash of personalities can truthfully be called "peacemaker" or "son of God." Jesus is quite right in this appraisal of life actions based upon proper motives and criteria. The completely mature parent is not one who separates antagonizing forces, only to leave the tension between the children unresolved. Rather, the mature father or mother is the one who appraises the situation wisely and resolves all tensions by skillfully maneuvering the two points of view into a position of satisfying compromise in which both parties can agree yet "save face." Once more we see Jesus portraying an attitude of

God as a characteristic of the mature man. Fortunate is he who possesses such attributes as the by-product of intimate communion with the heavenly Father.

(viii) "Blessed are those who are persecuted for righteousness' sake, for theirs is the kingdom of heaven. Blessed are you when men revile you and persecute you and utter all kinds of evil against you falsely on my account. Rejoice and be glad, for your reward is great in heaven, for so men persecuted the prophets who were before you."

For Jesus, he who returned good for ill, love for hate, suffering for anger was truly blessed. This type of response he regarded as his experience of God's way of responding to mankind and to him. That which was good for the Father was good for the Father's sons, among whom he counted himself. Of course, one must be in the right; and more than that, one must have the spiritual quality necessary to love sincerely those who persecuted one. There is no place in this concept for one with a martyr complex. Only those whose personal integrity is at stake can long endure persistent periods of persecution. Yet, says Jesus, even those with such integrity must not fret, for the prophets of old were persecuted also. Later on in his life Jesus was likewise to share in such persecution experiences and to personify in those moments his own teaching and faith. Apparently such steadfastness was for Jesus evidence of one's determined faith in God. Jesus taught as he believed and lived his faith. In this he is unique among his fellow religionists of all ages. Others spoke of ideals and recognized human weaknesses but in their own living failed to incarnate their messages. Jesus spoke of human potentialities and proceeded to reveal how man could attain such abundant living, not only by his message but through his own exemplary life.

This was no unattainable idealism. Rather, it was the revelation of man's individual potentiality. In Jesus' faith, all men could attain God-likeness; for Jesus said, "You, therefore, must become perfect as your heavenly Father is perfect."

(2) You have heard that it was said, "You shall love your neighbor and hate your enemy." But I say to you, Love your enemies and pray for those who persecute you, so that you may be sons of your Father who is in heaven; for he makes his sun rise on the evil and on the good, and sends rain on the just and on the unjust. For if you love those who love you, what reward have you? Do not even the tax collectors do the same? And if you salute only your brethren, what more are you doing than others? Do not even the Gentiles do the same? You, therefore, must be perfect, as your heavenly Father is perfect. (Matthew 5:43-48; cf. Luke 6:32-36)

The important passage in this selection is "He [God] makes his sun rise on the evil and on the good, and sends rain on the just and on the unjust." Here we look further into the faith of Jesus. From life he had learned that to allow men to do and to say what they wished would lead only to the self-rewarding of some and the self-reprisals of others. Human beings tend to love those who reciprocate and to hate those who treat them spitefully. Yet Jesus soon learned that God did not act that way. It appeared to be characteristic of God's own personality to remain steadfastly a compassionate Being whose blessings were showered upon both the just and the unjust, the good and the evil. In childlike fashion, Jesus submitted himself to the Father's Will in order to learn from Him the joy and peace that comes when one is truly parental and filial.

As Jesus had found eternal life in sonship by having the mind of God, so he desired that that same mind be found in every man, beginning with his disciples (cf. Paul in I Corinthians 2:16*b* and Philippians 2:5). Conscious of the happiness he had received by living in harmony with the spirit of the Father, he yearned to draw his disciples into the same happiness combining the favor of God with likeness unto God and manifesting itself in love. It is the necessary corollary of their being sons of the Father, since it is in conduct alone that the fullest manifestation of the filial relationship is revealed. Love fosters faith. As

The Faith He Shared

Jesus saw God loving all men in bestowing His gifts, so Jesus had faith to believe that his own gifts of "the Way, the Truth, and the Life" would bestow a quality to the lives of all those who had the faith to follow and to learn from him.

From the time of Amos of Tekoa to the present day, all thoughtful men have realized that a God who is Himself morally perfect must demand, or at least expect, moral perfection from His children and worshippers. As a son seeks to be as perfect and mature as his father, so Jesus conceived the son of God as seeking the perfection and maturity of the Divine Father. As he himself had chosen this for his standard of life, so he besought his disciples to accept nothing short of the full ideal as it is in God, the Father. This is both the gift and the responsibility of sonship as Jesus perceived it for himself and for each individual.

> (3) For no good tree bears bad fruit, nor again does a bad tree bear good fruit; for each tree is known by its own fruit. For figs are not gathered from thorns, nor are grapes picked from a bramble bush. The good man out of the good treasure of his heart produces good, and the evil man out of his evil treasure produces evil; for out of the abundance of the heart his mouth speaks. (Luke 6:43–45; cf. Matthew 7:16–21, 12:33–35)

The influence a man manifests in words, deeds and attitudes originates in the very nature of his being, and to the degree of his maturity. Man may struggle to act and masquerade before his compatriots and strangers, but unconsciously his true personality will betray itself in the little subtle acts and attitudes which he has failed to bring under discipline. There is no perfect actor. There is no complete incarnation. It were better, by far, that a man live naturally and informally among his brethren in order that his true character may find full expression for better or for worse. Only then could a man be true to himself; and his fellows would judge and forgive him justly. In the presence of such sincerity and integrity God challenges, forgives, redeems and guides the soul of that individual unto eternal life. To give evidence of insincerity and evil intent, no matter how respectably clothed, reveals a certain defilement of the soul. Jesus said, "Why do you call me 'Lord, Lord,' and not do what I tell you?" (Luke 6:46.)

The faith of Jesus shines forth in all its simplicity and purity in this urgent plea for personal integrity. The sincere son of God who like Jesus seeks to do the Father's Will will unconsciously radiate a quality of life which will manifest his filial relationship to the Father in spirit and substance. Only thus can one know and be sure of the true character of man at its best. Witness the life of Jesus himself at this point.

> (4) At that time Jesus declared, "I thank thee, Father, Lord of heaven and earth, that thou hast hidden these things from the wise and understanding and revealed them to babes; yea, Father, for such was thy gracious will. All things have been delivered to me by my Father; and no one knows the Son except the Father, and no one knows the Father, except the Son and any one to whom the Son chooses to reveal him." (Matthew 11:25–27; cf. Luke 10:21–22)

In this impromptu prayer Jesus gave us another glimpse of his faith. Here he revealed that he believed he had laid hold upon what he preferred to call "a revelation of divine truth" which had escaped the insights and wisdom of the intelligent and learned inhabitants. Yet Jesus apparently believed that this spiritual discernment can be grasped and understood by the most common and unpretentious person who allows himself to become spiritually sensitive. One is reminded of Jesus' remark to the Apostle Peter upon the latter's confession of faith (cf. Matthew 16:17). Jesus appears to intimate that divine wisdom and knowledge at its best comes by revelation, imparted by deity, and is spiritually discerned by those dedicated persons who submit completely to divine influences. This is the characteristic Hebraic-Jewish attitude toward man's efforts in thought and insight: true wisdom is acquired by divine revelation rather than by human philosophical questing. Tradition holds that Jesus regarded himself the first recipient and sole mediator of divine wisdom to the rest of his and to all succeeding generations of mankind.

(5) Then turning to the disciples he said privately, "Blessed are the eyes which see what you see! For I tell you that many prophets and kings desired to see what you see, and did not see it, and to hear what you hear, and did not hear it." (Luke 10:23-24; cf. Matthew 13:16-17)

The Lucan rendition of this passage most likely reflects the mind of Jesus on this matter. Matthew has taken the quotation and placed it in a new or another setting which caused him to make or to record several minor textual changes, especially in Matthew 13:16, which have completely altered the most likely original sense of the passage.

Undoubtedly Jesus meant for his audience to take him literally concerning his reference to eyes and ears, to seeing and hearing. But whether taken thus, or with spiritual connotations, the truth still can be grasped. It is this: that which even the most spiritually sensitive souls of the past had difficulty in perceiving is available to all who allow their souls to see and hear the voice of God. And what is this that they will hear and see? Why, it is the proclamation and the unfolding reality of the kingdom of God, i.e., the good news of eternal life within the individual and the society. To every child of God there is the potential opportunity to possess that quality of life that is fulfilling, satisfying, abundant and God-like. Of this life Jesus had become increasingly aware throughout his own experience. It therefore became his belief that all mankind, whatever the nation, the race, the class, the creed, could possess this quality of life also.

(6) Ask, and it will be given you; seek and you will find; knock, and it will be opened to you. For every one who asks

receives, and he who seeks finds, and to him who knocks it will be opened. Or what man of you, if his son asks him for a loaf, will give him a stone? Or if he asks for a fish, will give him a serpent? If you then, who are evil, know how to give good gifts to your children, how much more will your Father who is in heaven give good things to those who ask him? (Matthew 7:7–11; cf. Luke 11:9–13)

This great passage has had many homiletic interpretations, but our chief concern at this juncture is to discover what we can learn of Jesus' faith. We see Jesus' most certain fact of faith: God is his Father. He lived consciously in the atmosphere of that Father's goodness and love. He could not conceive of that Father being less wise and less kind than any human parent; for "if you then, who are evil, know how to give good gifts to your children, and how much more will your Father who is in heaven give good things to those who ask him?" Even the most rascally of men would be honest and kind in dealing with the request of his own child. How much more so is this true of the Heavenly Father! It is good to note that Jesus did not recognize the sinfulness of human nature; rather, he would point out simply the fact that men are imperfect both in motive and in action. But there does not appear any trace of a doctrine of original sin or inherited transgression.

This passage is not to be understood on this wise: if the parent gives food to the child asking for it, in like manner, God will give you food if you will but ask for it. On the contrary, it should be understood as meaning *as surely* as a parent will give food to a child asking for it, *so surely* will God give his gifts to those who ask. Moreover, these good things include both the "spiritual" (of Luke's Gospel) and the necessary "material" . . . both referring to the essentials, or bare necessities, of life. Jesus himself lived on these bare necessities of life and found them adequate. He had no definite habitat which he could call his own; he had no constant food supply by which he could feed himself; his clothes were well worn but in no sense ragged. The

The Faith He Shared

Father supplied the essentials of daily living, and Jesus was satisfied.

(7) When the unclean spirit has gone out of a man, he passes through waterless places seeking rest, but he finds none. Then he says, "I will return to my house from which I came." And when he comes he finds it empty, swept, and put in order. Then he goes and brings with him seven other spirits more evil than himself, and they enter and dwell there; and the last state of that man becomes worse than the first. So shall it be also with this evil generation. (Matthew 12:43-45; cf. Luke 11:24-26)

    The saying reflects the first century in terms of Jewish beliefs concerning demons and demon possession. It raises the question of Jesus' own attitudes toward belief in demons. Most Christians raise no question when this matter is discussed with Jesus' contemporaries in mind, but their high regard for Jesus refuses to allow them to place Jesus that completely in his own generation. For the average church member, Jesus must be "eternal" and therefore a sharer of twentieth-century thinking; and since demon possession is not a part of present-day thinking or beliefs, therefore Jesus could not have partaken of such antiquated concepts, even though he speaks at times as though he did. We must, however, allow Jesus to speak for himself, his fellow men and his own day. Belief in demons is the evidence of man's search, in the first Christian century, to explain difficulties which could not find any other explanation in that day but which have come to have innumerable explanations in this latter day.

    Assuming their explanation in terms of demons and demon possession, what is Jesus trying to say in this passage? It would appear that he would have his hearers believe that exorcism by itself was not sufficient. To drive out one or many demons with the hope of restoring the victim to a normal condition was only to leave things exactly as they were before the demon took possession: a deficient soul devoid of its rightful heritage and forgetful of its divine potentiality. If the demon was to be kept out, something must replace its habitation, lest its return cause further damage to the human being. For Jesus, God alone has the power to drive out the demon(s) and He alone must replace it (or them). This brings to mind Paul's comment in I Corinthians 3:16: "Do you not know that you are God's temple and that God's Spirit dwells in you?" (cf. II Corinthians 6:16 and Ephesians 2:22). Putting this into language more conducive to present-day understanding, Jesus was saying that our old obsessions, fears, complexes and desires must be replaced by new convictions, loyalties, affections, and hopes.

> (8) And do not fear those who kill the body but cannot kill the soul; rather fear him who can destroy both soul and body in hell. Are not two sparrows sold for a penny? And not one of them will fall to the ground without your Father's will. But even the hairs of your head are all numbered. Fear not, therefore; you are of more value than many sparrows. (Matthew 10:28-31; cf. Luke 12:4-7)

He who can destroy the soul is the real danger in life. We are urged not to worry or be frightened about physical danger, for that is all that persecution at its worst can threaten. Jesus promised no physical protection by God. Whatever physical harm comes to a son of God comes in the full knowledge of the Father. Fear should be reserved for spiritual perils. Anything which can injure a man's spiritual life is far more terrible than that which harms his physical being. God is more than creator; He is Father. He is interested in everything that affects His creatures (e.g., every sparrow that falls, that is sold, but much more than that, every son of God who falls, who is sold into slavery). Therefore God has great interest in man's destiny. This was Jesus' concept of a protecting and caring Father.

> (9) He went on his way through towns and villages, teaching, and journeying toward Jerusalem. And some one said

The Faith He Shared

to him, "Lord, will those who are saved be few?" And he said to them, "Strive to enter by the narrow door; for many, I tell you, will seek to enter and will not be able. When once the householder has risen up and shut the door, you will begin to stand outside and to knock at the door, saying, 'Lord, open to us.' He will answer you, 'I do not know where you come from.' Then you will begin to say, 'We ate and drank in your presence, and you taught in our streets.' But he will say, 'I tell you, I do not know where you come from; depart from me, all you workers of iniquity!' There you will weep and gnash your teeth, when you see Abraham and Isaac and Jacob and all the prophets in the kingdom of God and you yourselves thrust out. And men will come from east and west, and from north and south, and sit at table in the kingdom of God. And behold, some are last who will be first, and some are first who will be last." (Luke 13:22–30)

This passage in Luke has no consecutive parallel in the Gospel according to Matthew (cf. 7:13 ff., 25:10–12, 7:22 ff., 8:11–12). Luke, however, has undoubtedly sought to share Jesus' ideas on the subject of salvation and on the number of fortunate souls who are to be saved. The question is age-old. It almost presupposes that redemption depends in some mysterious way upon favoritism of God rather than upon His Love. But this is not a matter of either claiming sonship to Abraham or abandoning all hope for mankind. Jesus intimated that he believed, on the basis of his own experience, that the way of salvation was a door which God opens and man enters. It appears that Jesus regarded God alone as the opener of this door. This is the opposite of the apocalyptic reference in Revelation 3:20 of a later day, where the Christ is portrayed as awaiting man's initiative to open the door.

Entry into the way of salvation can be made only in the presence and with the assistance of God. The entrance is portrayed as narrow; one struggles in rather than strolls in. It would appear that Jesus believed that if men failed to enter, it was due not to God's arbitrariness but to man's own unwillingness.

In verses 25-27, we note an eschatological motive that is strange and at times repugnant to us. The first-century Palestinian Jew believed that the world might come to an end within the day, week, month or year. He believed that it was within God's jurisdiction; this placed some sort of a time limit upon the opportunity for repentance and salvation. When the door is ultimately closed, many shall knock, to find it shut (forever?).

On the privileged side of the door is light, life, joy and peace. The patriarchs and the prophets who symbolize the righteous of each generation are portrayed as sharing in the Kingdom, perhaps sitting down to the great messianic banquet which the Jews imagined would take place in the Kingdom at its coming. Outside, where the less fortunate stand in dismay, regret, and anger, there is darkness and despair, symbols and actualities of those hopeless souls. There appears to be no mention here of any special punishment for these recalcitrants. They are portrayed as suffering sufficiently in the loss of what might have been theirs.

For Jesus, there can be no special privilege for any man. The fate of man, if we may call it such, depended upon his response to the Will of God: a matter of repentance and submission to God. The reference to those from the east and west, from north and south, appears to reveal that Jesus believed that the Gentiles have already shown traits worthy of salvation, and it was his faith that God has always accepted their witness and loyalty, rewarding them likewise with eternal life. This is definite evidence of Jesus' universal faith, which took decades for his followers to discover and accept.

(10) He said to them, "Because of your little faith. For truly, I say to you, if you have faith as a grain of mustard seed, you will say to this mountain, 'Move hence to yonder place,' and it will move; and nothing will be impossible to you."
(Matthew 17:20)

The Faith He Shared

The apostles said to the Lord, "Increase our faith!" And the Lord said, "If you had faith as a grain of mustard seed, you could say to this sycamine tree, 'Be rooted up, and be planted in the sea,' and it would obey you." (Luke 17:5-6; cf. Mark 11:23)

The mere contextual settings for these passages reveal a confused tradition concerning this saying of Jesus. Mark 11:23 is a portion of the story about the withering of the barren fig tree. Matthew 17:20 is to be found in the story of the cure of the epileptic boy, replacing the original reply of Jesus as recorded in Mark 9:29. Luke 17:5-6 appears in quite a different form; the mountain has been replaced by a tree that is planted in the sea. In this, I Corinthians 13:2 appears to support the Mark and Matthew versions of the account. Of course, there is always the possibility that Jesus repeated his teachings with variations.

In the presence of such great faith as Jesus exhibited, the disciples appeared to lack faith. Timidity characterized the loyal followers of Jesus. His great personality and religious faith had covered them with uncertainty and fear. His insistence upon their unlimited readiness to forgive wrongs caused them to think that he was urging them beyond their ability and potentiality. Jesus appeared to reply that in his experience it was not a matter of quantity of faith; rather, it was a matter of quality. The smallest quantity of quality-faith was capable of accomplishing the seemingly impossible: i.e., as impossible as the removal of a mountain, or the transplanting of a tree into the midst of the sea. This saying reminds one of Jesus' comment concerning the camel and the eye of a needle (Mark 10:25, Matthew 19:24, Luke 18:25).

It is part of Jesus' inherent faith that mankind, as well as he, can achieve by a simple act of genuine faith life adjustments, improvements and corrections that seem to be impossible and absurd. Such an act of will and trust calls forth heroic spirits, not manipulators of seeming miracles. To act in and by faith with such abandonment takes the strength of courageous men who have no thought for their bodies but much for their souls. This Jesus had. Moreover, he assumed and expected it of all mankind.

From L

(11) And behold, a lawyer stood up to put him to the test, saying, "Teacher, what shall I do to inherit eternal life?" He said to him, "What is written in the law? How do you read?" And he answered, "You shall love the Lord your God with all your heart, and with all your soul, and with all your strength, and with all your mind; and your neighbor as yourself." And he said to him, "You have answered right; do this, and you will live." (Luke 10:25–28)

This passage appears to be a distinct Lucan account of an incident which may find a parallel, or another version, in Mark 12:28–31(34). Luke apparently thought so, for he fails to incorporate these verses from Mark into his Gospel. Luke appears to be more interested, however, in the replies of the lawyer and Jesus; that is, he is not concerned with Jesus' choice of the two particular commandments. Perhaps Luke was more concerned with preparing the context for the parable of the Good Samaritan. Therefore, he pointed his account toward the question: "Who is my neighbor?" Our interest in this passage, however, is to be found in Jesus' reply to the lawyer's choice of commandments: "You have answered right; do this, and you will live."

This is an opportunity to study Jesus' attitude toward salvation (assuming, of course, that he was speaking of a redeemed life when he said, "You will live"). Did Jesus mean to imply that he agreed with the pharisaic beliefs of his day: i.e., obey the letter of the law and by some miraculous happenstance you are "saved"? Taking it literally, one might very well get the impression that Jesus believed in salvation by works. We are led, however, to another conclusion in the matter as soon as we seek to define the "works" involved in loving God and one's neighbor. To love God, as Jesus apparently interpreted the phrase, meant a certain blending of respect for and of submission to God into a spiritual fellowship of kindred spirits. Thus it would appear that Jesus believed that as soon as theories, points of view and attitudes were actually and sincerely put into practice, the result would be life at its best. This would cause one to infer that Jesus assumed that people knew what they believed but failed to act in faith upon that belief, and therefore failed to share in the new life of the spirit.

This is a point which man has been slow to recognize in terms of Jesus himself. Unlike the other great founders of the world's religions, Jesus lived the message he preached. All that he required of and urged upon others, he had demanded and experienced for himself. He was sharing his faith as he had found it and as he believed it to be: the key to righteous living and true happiness. Abundant living is the adventure of daily living "as though" the ideal kingdom was already here, exercising righteous motives "as though" they were the common possession of all citizens. What Jesus was trying to say was this: the life you see me living is the way of life as it is intended by God, as it will be lived in the Kingdom, as it can be participated in now, if individuals will only lay hold upon it in faith.

(12) While he was speaking, a Pharisee asked him to dine with him; so he went in and sat at table. The Pharisee was astonished to see that he did not first wash before dinner. And the Lord said to him, "Now you Pharisees cleanse the outside of the cup and of the dish, but inside you are full of extortion and wickedness. You fools! Did not he who made the outside make the inside also? But give for alms those things which are within; and behold, everything is clean for you." (Luke 11:37–41)

As he went away from there, the scribes and the Pharisees began to press him hard, and to provoke him to speak of many things, lying in wait for him, to catch at something he might say.

In the meantime, when so many thousands of the multitude had gathered together that they trod upon one another, he began to say to his disciples first, "Beware of the leaven of the Pharisees, which is hypocrisy." (Luke 11:53–12:1)

The omitted passage (Luke 11:42–52) in the above account contains the Q collection of woes against the scribes and Pharisees. Scholars appear to accept the above disconnected references as a complete and self-contained story into which Luke has inserted some other traditional material.

What is Jesus seeking to say in this passage? The message is simply this: if the heart is pure, then the whole man is pure. Jesus believed that the only way to correct the outer character and actions of a person was to change his motives, i.e., his heart. Can this be the philosophic solution to man's problems as Jesus has thought it through? Did Jesus believe that all sin resulted from wrong or false motivations? Was Jesus implying that man needed only to correct his heart and then new life would result, brotherhood would be achieved and the kingdom of God would manifest itself in an earthly context? It would appear to be almost that simple until we realize, as Jesus did, what is involved in the changing or correcting of the hearts or motives of men. This is not achieved by mere re-education of the mind, nor is it by wishful thinking. We discover elsewhere (cf. Mark 14:36) that Jesus has thought for some time about this matter. For him, man's submissiveness to the will of God at every moment of decision would result ultimately in a spiritual likeness or unity which is reflected in the fourth Gospel's interpretation of Jesus' godlikeness (cf. "I and the Father are one"—John 10:30) and in Paul's testimony of his own experience ("It is no longer I who live, but Christ who lives in me"—Galatians 2:20), as well as in Paul's teachings ("Join in imitating me, and mark those who live as you have an example in us"—Philippians 3:17; cf. Ephesians 5:1).

(13) One of the multitude said to him, "Teacher, bid my brother divide the inheritance with me." But he said to him, "Man, who made me a judge or divider over you?" But he said to them, "Take heed, and beware of all covetousness; for a man's life does not consist in the abundance of his possessions." And he told them a parable, saying, "The land of a rich man brought forth plentifully; and he thought to himself, 'What shall I do, for I have nowhere to store my crops?' And he said, 'I will do this: I will pull down my barns, and build larger ones; and there I will store all my grain and my goods. And I will say to my soul, Soul, you have ample goods laid up for many years; take your ease, eat, drink, be merry.' But God said to him, 'Fool! This night your soul is required of you; and the things you have prepared, whose will they be?' So is he who lays up treasure for himself, and is not rich toward God." (Luke 12:13–21)

We should note first that Jesus appears to ignore the circumstances of the case, the injustice involved, or the application of law. The significant factor as Jesus saw it was the fact that two men, children of the same God, members of the same faith, citizens of the same nation or community, are separated and antagonistic toward each other. What was needed was not justice brought to bear, nor even the application of law with its accompanying punishment for illegalities. Rather, these two individuals, as well as the multitude present, needed to feel the disgrace and shame of such an occasion.

Jesus believed that when men are made to realize and feel this disgrace, they will experience a strong sense of humility and the two individuals will act in a more brotherly way. They will seek to settle the matter not so much on the basis of tolerant justice as merciful amiability. What was needed in the situation as Jesus saw it was the elimination of that which made for the dispute. We see man selfishly seeking the material things in life as the chief means to happiness. Jesus' reply was that he who would participate in life at its fullness must learn the hard truth of experience; i.e., the acquisition of material goods does not secure for the individual either happiness or a richer quality of life. This general principle has been made most emphatic in the parable of the rich fool (verses 16–21). The concluding verse supplies a moral to the story.

> (14) There were some present at that very time who told him of the Galileans whose blood Pilate had mingled with their sacrifices. And he answered them, "Do you think that these Galileans were worse sinners than all the other Galileans, because they suffered thus? I tell you, No; but unless you repent you will all likewise perish. Or those eighteen upon whom the tower in Siloam fell and killed them, do you think that they were worse offenders than all the others who dwelt in Jerusalem? I tell you, No; but unless you repent you will all likewise perish."
> And he told this parable: "A man had a fig tree planted in his vineyard; and he came seeking fruit on it and found none. And he said to the vinedresser, 'Lo, these three years I have come seeking fruit on this fig tree, and I find none. Cut it down; why should it use up the ground?' And he answered him, 'Let it alone, sir, this year also, till I dig about it and put on manure. And if it bears fruit next year, well and good; but if not, you can cut it down.'" (Luke 13:1–9)

This passage is primarily concerned with the matter of urgency in securing the new life. The motive for confronting Jesus with the incident is unknown. Perhaps the story was told in the hope that it would rouse Jesus to respond in some seditious manner. The truth of the matter is that Jesus avoided the issues raised by their questions and promptly forced his own message upon them. He apparently was aware of their motives. He did not even care to indulge in a comment on the problem of suffering into which the questions might easily have led. He moved the discussion, however, completely out of context and spent the time of the audience in expounding the urgency of the gospel.

The records persistently show Jesus to be a man of great concern and urgency. His "good news" was the symptom of anxiety. As a trumpet blaring in the darkness, the gospel called for repentance and self-effacement in view of what was considered the ending of this age or world. Jesus appears to have a gloomy outlook upon the trends of and in society as he viewed it. We cannot and must not say, however, that he was a pessimist or a defeatist. Nevertheless, he saw his day and generation "riding for a fall."

In this attitude we see Jesus' concept of history, Providence and destiny. It is quite evident that Jesus believed in a philosophy of history which cannot be called "progress." The world, from his point of view, was not getting better and better. Yet he would be the last to say that it lacked the potentialities to become such, either by their own efforts or by out-and-out deific intervention. In fact, this passage reveals the earnest efforts of Jesus to overcome the handicap of his generation at this very point. Jesus appears to be saying: Consider the past! Learn from history! There was Noah and the Flood; there was Sodom and Gomorrah in the days of Abraham and Lot. There are potentialities for improvement in every man and nation, every generation and age. Every individual, whatever his environmental circumstances, is potentially a son of God. Every society holds within its grasp the seeds of the Kingdom of God on earth.

Jesus' concern was with his own generation, of course. The drive of his soul was to "save" *his* generation from sure disaster. The people did not see the symptoms of the coming doom. The unexpected in life always seems to come when man least expects it and is least prepared to face it triumphantly. When Jesus' "good news" is truly discerned by the sincere and sensitive soul, such preparedness is achieved and such triumph is experienced. Jesus knew this in his own inner being; and the author of the fourth Gospel, recognizing this fact, sought to express it by having Jesus say: "I have overcome the world" (John 16:33). For Jesus it was a marvelous spiritual experience and victory. He had been a participator in this miracle; he believed that each individual could likewise participate in the marvelous joy of this abundant life.

The central point of this passage, therefore, appears to be this: God is both just and merciful, both disciplinary and loving, truly parental, not paternal! If God had dealt with Israel according to strict justice, Israel would have perished long ago. That, however, was not the case. In divine love God extended to Israel another chance.

> (15) And he said, "There was a man who had two sons; and the younger of them said to his father, 'Father, give me the share of property that falls to me.' And he divided his living between them. Not many days later, the younger son gathered all he had and took his journey into a far country, and there he squandered his property in loose living. And when he had spent everything, a great famine arose in that country, and he began to be in want. So he went and joined himself to one of the citizens of that country, who sent him into his fields to feed swine. And he would gladly have fed on the pods that the swine ate; and no one gave him anything. But when he came to himself he said, 'How many of my father's hired servants have bread enough and to spare, but I perish here with hunger! I will arise and go to my father, and I will say to him, "Father, I have sinned against heaven and before you; I am no longer worthy to be called your son; treat me as one of your hired servants."' And he arose and came to his father. But while he was yet at a distance, his father saw him and had compassion, and ran and embraced him and kissed him. And the son said to him, 'Father, I have sinned against heaven and before you; I am no longer worthy to be called your son.' But the father said to his servants, 'Bring quickly the best robe, and put it on

The Faith He Shared

him; and put a ring on his hand, and shoes on his feet; and bring the fatted calf and kill it, and let us eat and make merry; for this my son was dead, and is alive again; he was lost, and is found.' And they began to make merry.

"Now his elder son was in the field; and as he came and drew near to the house, he heard music and dancing. And he called one of the servants and asked what this meant. And he said to him, 'Your brother has come, and your father has killed the fatted calf, because he has received him safe and sound.' But he was angry and refused to go in. His father came out and entreated him, but he answered his father, 'Lo, these many years I have served you, and I never disobeyed your command; yet you never gave me a kid, that I might make merry with my friends. But when this son of yours came, who has devoured your living with harlots, you killed for him the fatted calf!' And he said to him, 'Son, you are always with me, and all that is mine is yours. It was fitting to make merry and be glad, for this your brother was dead, and is alive; he was lost, and is found.'" (Luke 15:11-32)

This famous parable was chosen to represent the parabolic trilogy which forms the fifteenth chapter of the Gospel according to Luke. There appears to be one basic belief upon which all the teachings gathered in Luke 15-19 are established: that God wills that the sinner should be redeemed, sooner or later, depending upon the willful activity of the sinner. Jesus appears to be concerned with the publicans and sinners not merely from humanitarian interest and enthusiasm, as would be expected or surmised, but rather from a deep awareness of an affinity to the Divine Will for the individual. This collection of teachings reveals a vigorous and firm conviction that God not only wills to restore sinners but wills to redeem them in a particular way, the way of merciful love. The belief assumed by Jesus is that God took the initiative in ferreting out the sinner, and in so enveloping him with mercy that in true repentance he would submit his will to the Divine Will, and would receive God's promised eternal life.

Jesus, in the parable before us, appears to be making two important revelations of his own personal faith. (i) The first has already been developed in pointing up the care and concern God has for the sinner, and the joy with which He receives each repentant sinner back into His love and fellowship. (ii) The other is the subtle inference that knowledge of the existence of God's undeserved mercy towards the sinner would motivate the outcast to repent of his wrongdoing and seek divine forgiveness for his soul.

Many Christian scholars and laymen refuse even to recognize the theological problem which this parable poses—undoubtedly because of preconceived convictions regarding the Christian doctrine of salvation. Yet the problem must be faced candidly. The problem is this: If Jesus' teaching reflects his personal faith, as well as any connotations of divine purpose, then where does the sacrificial death of Jesus fit into the divine scheme of redemption? Ignoring the fact of Jesus' crucifixion and death, ignoring the orthodox doctrines of the Christian Church concerning the Passion, one is confronted by the fact that in Jesus' teaching and faith there is no need for a physical sacrifice to justify man's soul. Jesus' scheme of salvation needs no element of sacrifice, nonhuman or human. In defense of the traditional position of the Church in this matter, some scholars have tried to keep their orthodoxy intact by claiming (*a*) that Jesus was not attempting a full exposition of his doctrine of atonement in this parable, and (*b*) that the Church's doctrine of atonement is based upon more evidence than is supplied in this parable. We are convinced by the evidence, however, that any doctrine of atonement which in any way weakens or nullifies the basic principles laid down in this parable by Jesus himself has no chance of survival.

(16) There was a rich man, who was clothed in purple and fine linen and who feasted sumptuously every day. And at

his gate lay a poor man named Lazarus, full of sores, who desired to be fed with what fell from the rich man's table; moreover the dogs came and licked his sores. The poor man died and was carried by the angels to Abraham's bosom. The rich man also died and was buried; and in Hades, being in torment, he lifted up his eyes, and saw Abraham far off and Lazarus in his bosom. And he called out, "Father Abraham, have mercy upon me, and send Lazarus to dip the end of his finger in water and cool my tongue; for I am in anguish in this flame." But Abraham said, "Son, remember that you in your lifetime received your good things, and Lazarus in like manner evil things; but now he is comforted here, and you are in anguish. And besides all this, between us and you a great chasm has been fixed, in order that those who would pass from here to you may not be able, and none may cross from there to us." And he said, "Then I beg you, father, to send him to my father's house, for I have five brothers, so that he may warn them, lest they also come into this place of torment." But Abraham said, "They have Moses and the prophets; let them hear them." And he said, "No, father Abraham; but if some one goes to them from the dead, they will repent." He said to him, "If they do not hear Moses and the prophets, neither will they be convinced if some one should rise from the dead." (Luke 16:19–31)

This parable has caused great speculation among its innumerable readers. Granted that it is a parable, or a delightful story, the question that is almost always raised is: Did Jesus unconsciously reveal his mental concepts of the nether-regions when he described the plights of the rich man and Lazarus? Scholarship has preferred to believe that Jesus was adapting a popular tale for his own ends. When we seek to discover Jesus' purpose for relating this particular parable, we notice that he was more concerned with emphasizing the fact that there was a future life than he was with verifying the descriptions of that life. Jesus' point in the teaching of this parable was that the Torah and the Prophets were authority enough for anyone in the first century to believe in life after death. Could it be that these particular scriptures were the fountain source of his own belief in life after death? The parable appears to be directed toward the Sadducees and their disbelief in life hereafter. Therefore, his chief concern was guiding them in their thinking to the discovery of the truth he proclaimed: there *is* life after death. Beyond that proclamation there is no conscious attempt made to establish the details of that other world, either in physical description or in moral quality.

A secondary revelation of Jesus' faith is seen in his customary portrayal of God as one who expects men not only to be merciful and understanding toward the morally frail, but to be generous and gracious to the victims of poverty, sickness and other ills that befall mankind.

> (17) He also told this parable to some who trusted in themselves that they were righteous and despised others: "Two men went up into the temple to pray, one a Pharisee and the other a tax collector. The Pharisee stood and prayed thus with himself, 'God, I thank thee that I am not like other men, extortioners, unjust, adulterers, or even like this tax collector. I fast twice a week, I give tithes of all that I get.' But the tax collector, standing far off, would not even lift up his eyes to heaven, but beat his breast, saying, 'God, be merciful to me a sinner!' I tell you, this man went down to his house justified rather than the other; for every one who exalts himself will be humbled, but he who humbles himself will be exalted." (Luke 18:9-14)

This rather famous parable reminds one of the elder brother in the parable of the Prodigal Son. We can assume that Jesus' portrayals of the Pharisee and the publican are genuine representations of two types of individuals. Jesus, however, was concerned chiefly with the attitudes of the two characters. One, the **Pharisee**, appears to be satisfied with his lot; he is interested only in maintaining his presently satisfying way of life. The other, the publican, reveals a sincere discontent with his place in life; he recognizes his sinfulness, his failure to live at his best. For Jesus, the latter goes away justified, saved, redeemed, because the future of his life will be determined by the attitude of the present, and this pointed toward improvement.

Dare we intimate Jesus' personal attitude toward life at this moment? In the light of Christian doctrine one is tempted to identify Jesus with the Pharisee in the parable. If Jesus be sinless, as his followers have always maintained, then he may very sincerely join the Pharisee in his prayer for the continuing of the present state of his soul. On the other hand, if we identify Jesus' personal attitude with that of the publican, we find the outcome to be a very different Jesus from that portrayed in traditional Christology. For Jesus to express an attitude of heaven-born discontent is to intimate that Jesus was a growing, evolving, progressing, improving personality that had not attained divine identity but, in his own words, "was *becoming* perfect as the heavenly Father is *perfect*" (cf. Matthew 5:48). Such a picture of the historic Jesus is one of the major convictions of this study.

One of the marks of divine quality is the humble recognition that there is room for continuing improvement, not the attitude of having attained already. The faith of Jesus appears to be founded upon the maintenance of a sense of shortcoming. Some people would stress the negative statement of this feeling, i.e., the sense of failure, of guilt, of downright sin. But this is not in keeping with Jesus' positive optimism. Jesus always saw the potentialities of personal lives rather than the shortcomings and the sins. This aspect of character appears to be the one Jesus himself maintained throughout his earthly life, and the type he expects of all those who would experience the abundant life as sons of God. The implications in connection with Jesus' faith-experience could cause a revolt in Christological thinking.

(18) And he said, "Take heed that you are not led astray; for many will come in my name, saying, 'I am he!' and, 'The

time is at hand!' Do not go after them. And when you hear of wars and tumults, do not be terrified; for this must first take place, but the end will not be at once."

Then he said to them, "Nation will rise against nation, and kingdom against kingdom; there will be great earthquakes, and in various places famines and pestilences; and there will be terrors and great signs from heaven." (Luke 21:8-11; cf. Mark 13:5-8)

There are those who believe these words are from "the little apocalypse" referred to in Eusebius' *Ecclesiastical History* (Bk. iii, v, 3) because the Marcan parallel (13:5-8) is definitely a part of that oracle. Just how much of this apocalyptic material in the Gospel is from Jesus has always been a question. Some of this apocalyptic material must be from the mind and lips of Jesus; else the early church would not be so free with its use in the records of Jesus (cf. Mark 13, Matthew 24 and Luke 21).

Allow this selection to echo at least the limited use of apocalyptic thought by Jesus, what does it reveal of his faith? (*a*) First, it demonstrates that he was a man of his own times, sharing the belief in the potential power of God to intervene in human history and to change the course of human events completely. Just how far Jesus went in formulating this concept in terms of material readjustments in relation to spiritual realignment is a moot question. There have been advocates of both emphases, but the actual position of Jesus was probably somewhere between the two extremes, and was mostly a combination of both. (*b*) Secondly, it reveals once again Jesus' utter faith in God as the all-powerful Creator whose will and purposes are good and meaningful. Jesus appears to have believed that God has a plan which is not always clear or complete in the comprehension of men. It is evident that Jesus believed that he, along with John the Baptist and others, had some definite part to play in the bringing into reality and practical fruition that divine hope. Yet, elsewhere (Matthew 24:36, Mark 13:32; cf. Acts 1:7) Jesus appears to be well aware of the fact that neither he nor any other human creature knew the plan sufficiently well to predict the day or the hour when the plan would take place. His public ministry, however, is the testimony of his staunch belief in the coming new day, which he and John the Baptist preferred to think of in the popular terms, as the Kingdom of God.

(19) A dispute also arose among them, which of them was to be regarded as the greatest. And he said to them, "The kings of the Gentiles exercise lordship over them; and those in authority over them are called benefactors. But not so with you; rather let the greatest among you become as the youngest, and the leader as one who serves. For which is the greater, one who sits at table, or one who serves? Is it the one who sits at table? But I am among you as one who serves.

"You are those who have continued with me in my trials; as my Father appointed a kingdom for me, so do I appoint for you that you may eat and drink at my table in my kingdom, and sit on thrones judging the twelve tribes of Israel." (Luke 22:24–30)

This passage appears to have come from a special source accessible to Luke. There are parallels to various portions of this saying; verses 24–26 are similar to Mark 10:42–45 (cf. Mark 9:33–37 and Luke 9:46–48) and verses 28–30 have a parallel in an M passage (Matthew 19:28). Verse 27 does not seem to have a companion passage.

Taken at its face value, this passage reveals a strange combination of humility and conceit—humility in the fact that he has come to minister and not to be ministered unto (and this sounds like the Jesus we see throughout the first three Gospels); conceit in the statement that it is *his* Kingdom and that *he* can give a portion, if not all, of the Kingdom not to all disciples but only to the Twelve (and this latter comment sounds more like the Jesus revealed in the fourth Gospel, so unlike the humble servant of the first three Gospels). This passage may therefore reveal one of the temptations of his soul which he mentioned here (v. 28): that he realized his utter dependence upon his Heavenly Father, yet his religious experience compelled him to feel that in some mysterious way he was after all the unique tool of the Father. The Kingdom was the Father's idea, but its supervision was Jesus' responsibility. The idea seems to have found ready acceptance in the thought of later Christian theology: (i) no kingdom was available for mankind before Jesus; (ii) Jesus was sent to establish the Kingdom; (iii) Jesus was not like other men, but was sent from heaven in a unique and supernatural way (cf. Virgin Birth in Matthew and Luke, and The Word Become Flesh in John); (iv) no one was saved outside the Kingdom; (v) Jesus was forced to preach the gospel in Sheol to bring the good people of past, pre-Christian eras into the Kingdom (cf. I Peter 4:6, 3:19); and (vi) Jesus was coming again to establish his Kingdom on earth in place of man's selfish and sinful present copy of the Kingdom.

Yet what does this passage actually reveal of Jesus' faith? First, Jesus appears to believe that God has given, appointed or assigned the Kingdom to his personal supervision. He felt totally responsible for its administration and character. He expected to share it with the Twelve, whom he had personally chosen, presumably with some divine guidance. They were to share all of the Kingdom's joys (e.g., the feasting), privileges and responsibilities (e.g., the thrones and judging). Second, it is quite evident that Jesus believed that he held an important position in the Kingdom. Perhaps it was self-esteem born of a great experience and of a feeling of deep responsibility in carrying out the Father's Will. We need not read into the passage any sense of conceit or bigotry. Jesus was probably extremely sincere in expressing his sense of obligation to the Father. He appears to feel that it was up to him to carry out the details of his Father's Will as it had been revealed to him. Third, there appears to be some evidence that Jesus believed in the matter of rewards and punishments. This may not be so much a matter of merits as of normal results. Jesus appears to be saying: Such faithfulness as you have shown in periods of temptations and trials has its by-products in joy and inner satisfaction as well as in an increased sense of privilege and responsibility. This was in no sense a matter of bartering or bookkeeping; rather, it was completely in the realm of spiritual experience and polity. Finally, the keynote of the passage is found in Jesus' use of the word "serve." Service is to be the attitude and motivation of life, not only for himself but for his followers who would participate in the Kingdom with him. Elsewhere (Matthew 20:28), Jesus stated this matter for himself in no uncertain terms: "even as the Son of man [Matthew's usual phrase meaning "I"] came not to be served, but to serve." On one occasion (Mark 9:35) he practically demands it of his followers: "If anyone would be first, he must be last of all and servant of all." Jesus stated the principle, put in rather general terms, as follows: "He who finds his life will lose it, and he who loses his life for my sake will find it" (Matthew 10:39).

From M

(20) You are the salt of the earth; but if salt has lost its taste, how shall its saltness be restored? It is no longer good for anything except to be thrown out and trodden under foot by men.

You are the light of the world. A city set on a hill cannot be hid. Nor do men light a lamp and put it under a bushel, but on a stand, and it gives light to all in the house. Let your light so shine before men, that they may see your good works and give glory to your Father who is in heaven. (Matthew 5:13–16)

This passage is clearly from the M source and may have been two distinct teachings originally, proclaimed on separate occasions. In saying, "You are the salt of the earth," and "You are the light of the world," Jesus was saying in so many words, "You are responsible to the Heavenly Father for the quality of life you live." All eyes are upon those individuals who publicly proclaim that they are living according to the Will of God. All humanity is seeking the answer to these two questions: What are the characteristics of the perfectly mature personality which the Deity desires for mankind? And how does one acquire or achieve that mature quality of being?

The first symbol, salt, is very revealing of Jesus' ideas concerning the child of God. One would assume that Jesus chose his symbols carefully. In choosing salt, he undoubtedly meant to imply that righteous children of God had the sterling qualities of the mineral in the constitution of their personalities. Salt has three basic characteristics connected with its place and significance in human usage: (i) *Salt brings out the best* in flavor and in quality of the substance, be it vegetable, meat, or fruit. (ii) *Salt preserves the best,* as in the case of salted meat and vegetables. (iii) *Salt is essential to life;* no creature of God can long endure without its savor. Thus we behold Jesus' estimation of God's children when their saltiness is manifested in their every word and action. God's children will be known for their environmental influence, enlightenment and encouragement. God's children will also be known for their embodiment of the good, the chaste, the truthful, the faithful and the respectful. His children will preserve those attributes of being which characterize the Godhead. Therein all of Jesus' disciples will manifest their master's superb personality and life. God's children of this quality are truly essential to the maintenance of some semblance of humanity. Jesus believed this was possible for each man, whatever his race, nationality, class or creed.

When we turn to the other symbol, light, we discover a different set of characteristics, but basically the same qualities are implied: (i) *Light disperses darkness,* even the darkness of evil, and reveals what is real, true and beautiful in its native simplicity. (ii) *Light cannot be hid;* it reveals its supreme qualities when its environment is darkest, blackest. (iii) *Light,* like salt, *is essential to life* and to the maintenance of God's intentions.

These particular passages reveal Jesus' conscious sense of per-

The Faith He Shared

sonal responsibility. He was aware of a divine trust being placed upon his own life; he was to live so that others may see God in and through him. If he was aware of this responsibility, how much more should they be aware of their like responsibility. The eyes of the world are upon both him and his followers. They dare not, they must not, fail mankind, who is hungering and thirsting after righteousness and peace.

There does not appear to be any conscious desire for self-glory. The teaching is almost naïve in its faith in humanity: be good in order that others may see the attributes of God in you and, in seeing God's likeness, fail to be cognizant of you. This would lead one to believe that Jesus actually thought human beings could and should approximate the character of the Deity. Yet we are driven to the conclusion that this was not a fallacy in Jesus' reasoning, but a mark of his faith that each individual human personality, however thwarted by physical or mental handicaps, was potentially capable of manifesting a character of divine quality.

This would reveal Jesus' fundamental belief in man. When taught how to respond to any combination of circumstances, man could and would develop slowly but surely into a likeness of divine personality. Thus we are reminded of his other teaching: "You, therefore, must become perfect, as your heavenly Father is perfect." Or as the King James version says: "Become ye perfect as your heavenly Father is perfect" (Matthew 5:48).

(21) Beware of practicing your piety before men in order to be seen by them; for then you will have no reward from your Father who is in heaven.

Thus, when you give alms, sound no trumpet before you, as the hypocrites do in the synagogues and in the streets, that they may be praised by men. Truly, I say to you, they have their reward. But when you give alms, do not let your left hand know what your right hand is doing, so that your alms may be in secret; and your Father who sees in secret will reward you. (Matthew 6:1–4)

This collection of selected teachings is introduced by the first verse. "Piety" will be used as a comprehensive term covering these three activities of almsgiving, prayer and fasting (cf. Matthew 6:1–8). Here Jesus was attacking the superficial worshipper. In Matthew 5:16, we saw what Jesus believed to be the true significance of piety: not self-glory, but the exaltation of God's spirit at work in men.

Beginning with verse 2 we have Jesus' approach to almsgiving. We are not to equate hypocrites with any party or class in Judaism; rather, we are to view all vain givers as self-seeking. They make their contributions to charity not to relieve distress but to buy popular approval or admiration. In that way, they get what they pay for. The deal is transacted. They have received in full what they paid for. For Jesus, almsgiving was a personal, and most often a secret, affair. Such generosity was known primarily to God. This was the only type of charity which Jesus believed God approved, because the giver sought nothing for himself. The one who shared his more fortunate circumstances with his less fortunate brother was seeking only to relieve the distress of his neighbor. We are called upon to be good for goodness' sake, because it is good to be good, and not in order to escape the disasters of "hell" or to receive the rewards of "heaven." Such an attitude towards almsgiving Jesus himself exercised in his daily living.

> (22) And when you pray, you must not be like the hypocrites; for they love to stand and pray in the synagogues and at the street corners, that they may be seen by men. Truly, I say to you, they have their reward. But when you pray, go into your room and shut the door and pray to your Father who is in secret; and your Father who sees in secret will reward you.
>
> And in praying do not heap up empty phrases as the Gentiles do; for they think that they will be heard for their many words. Do not be like them, for your Father knows what you need before you ask him. (Matthew 6:5–8)

The Faith He Shared

The second pious act selected was praying. Here Matthew has brought together at least three distinct sayings of Jesus (vv. 5-6, 7-8, and 9-13). We shall treat the first two selections together and then deal with the so-called "Lord's Prayer" later.

In verses 5 and 6 we see that Jesus' attitude toward private prayer was similar to that which he expressed in connection with almsgiving. Private prayer could be a wholesome and rewarding spiritual experience for the faithful soul, but it could also be an opportunity for hypocritical display for the impious individual. The hypocrite in religion wanted to be admired for his piety; the devotee went about his business of religious living without thought of personal aggrandizement.

Such an attitude reveals Jesus' own personal approach to prayer. Although at times he had near at hand Peter, James and John, Jesus usually "went apart to pray." For him to pray was "to be alone with God," uninterrupted by the noises of material existence. There, in the quiet recesses of his own soul as well as of his environment, he communed with his Heavenly Father: sharing joys and sorrows, seeking insights and vindications, basking in the spiritual fellowship of God's Presence, Love, Thought and Will. Like the young man in Hawthorne's story of "The Great Stone Face," the young boy became a man only to discover that he had unconsciously assimilated all the characteristics of his hero, the Old Man of the Mountain, and the young man's contemporaries recognized this startling fact and proclaimed him the incarnation of that hero.

In verses 7 and 8 another characteristic of Jesus' prayer life manifests itself. He was not given to "vain repetitions" or "much speaking." Prayer may be as long or short as the occasion warrants; Jesus had no fault to find with the length of prayers. His chief criticism appears to be regarding the use made of prayer time. Prayer for Jesus was neither one-way chatter upon the part of the devotee, nor the superstitious use of certain words, phrases and "prayers." In contrast with the Gentile, Jesus was dealing with one God whom he regarded as a Heavenly Father. For Jesus, this God already knew what the petitioner needed even before he asked. This was the way of God, Jesus believed. Yet this did not deter even Jesus from praying to the Heavenly Father. Jesus appeared to take nothing for granted; rather, he unconsciously set an example for his teaching. Of this Jesus' disciples became increasingly aware (cf. Luke 11:2-4). So we are introduced now to an appraisal and interpretation of the Lord's Prayer.

(23) Pray then like this:

>Our Father who art in heaven,
>Hallowed be thy name.
>Thy kingdom come,
>Thy will be done,
>   On earth as it is in heaven.
>Give us this day our daily bread;
>And forgive us our debts,
>   As we also have forgiven our debtors;
>And lead us not into temptation,
>   But deliver us from evil. (Matthew 6:9-13)

He was praying in a certain place, and when he ceased, one of his disciples said to him, "Lord, teach us to pray, as John taught his disciples." And he said to them, "When you pray, say:

"Father, hallowed be thy name. Thy kingdom come. Give us each day our daily bread; and forgive us our sins, for we ourselves forgive every one who is indebted to us; and lead us not into temptation." (Luke 11:1-4)

The setting for this model prayer is very much in dispute. No one will ever know when and under what circumstances these best known words of Jesus were spoken. Critics have chosen the Lucan form rather than the Matthean, for reason of its suggestive, impromptu, abbreviated sketch and seeming extemporaneousness. They contend that the Matthean form has about it a literary smoothness and an almost liturgical character suggestive

The Faith He Shared

of early Christian litany. (For these reasons we have cited both passages.)

Whatever the form or length, the sum and substance of the so-called "Lord's Prayer" is the same. Here we see a prayer of Jesus which is consciously didactic yet remains devotional and alive. It was a prayer prayed by Jesus. It sprung from the very depths of his deep religious experience. Every word, phrase and thought came out of the experience of Jesus.

In our exposition we shall follow the form found in the Gospel according to Matthew. *Our Father* refers to Jesus' central belief in God as a loving Heavenly Father: Father of Jesus, and the Father of us all. For all who call upon Him, He is "Our Father." *Who art in Heaven* presents the amazing fact that, for Jesus, God is always transcendent, apart from man, despite His apparent nearness. *Hallowed be thy name,* i.e., "revered be Thy character," refers to the holiness of God as Jesus perceived Him in traditional terms. *Thy Kingdom come.* This was the Gospel of Hope: together with all Jews, Jesus and his disciples prayed for the coming of the Kingdom of God, regardless of the manner in which each person conceived of its manifestation. Yet the means by which Jesus believed it would come was then *Thy will be done.* This is the law of human nature. The mind and will of the Father was to be matched with a reflecting mind and will of a devout son, *on earth as it is in heaven. Give us this day our daily bread* is a petition for sustenance and necessities, not luxuries. Although "your heavenly Father knows that you need them all" (Matthew 6:32, cf. Luke 12:30*b*), yet it is well to reveal the desires of your heart to Him and not cast up a barrier between yourself and God. *And forgive us our debts, as we also have forgiven our debtors.* The emphasis should be placed on the five words *as we also have forgiven,* for we can expect God to forgive only as we are forgiving. But it must be noted immediately that our forgiving is not the ground on which God bestows His forgiveness, but rather the ground on which man can receive and genuinely appreciate His forgiveness. Forgiveness is the first of God's gifts to men; therefore Jesus pointed out the primacy of forgiveness in the fellowship of sons of God. This is the passage which caused orthodox Christian theology of the past to cut off this prayer from the experience of Jesus and claim it for the disciples only. This unfortunate appraisal of it was based on the theoretical theology of the sinlessness of Jesus; and such misinterpretation hides the very soul of Jesus' personal piety from mankind. *And lead us not into temptation;* this phrase has been a stumblingblock for interpreters. They would not have God causing us to do wrong in accordance with His own will. Neither would they have God the originator of evil or temptation. But if one had the eyes with which to see and the ears with which to hear the truth of the statement, it would be comprehended very easily; it appears so simple, yet it is so complex. Jesus undoubtedly said these words with this thought in mind: A true son of God seeks to his utmost to do the will of his Father, and therefore, having complete faith in that Father to lead him ever forward along the road of life, he is urged to pray that the Father will not lead him into temptation but will keep the eyes of the son ever open to the snares of life. In the life of Jesus himself we see this prayer interpreted in what we called the "first" crisis. *But deliver us from evil* (or *the evil one*). As a child asks of its father protection and care from the harm of bad men and women, so Jesus conceived of the son of God as petitioning protection and care from his Heavenly Father. One was to ask for protection not only from evil people but from all evil. It was at this point that both renditions of the model prayer ended. The benediction *for thine is the kingdom and the power and the glory forever and ever, Amen,* is of very early origin, but scholars are quite certain that it had no part in the prayer as Jesus gave it to his followers.

(24) And when you fast, do not look dismal, like the hypocrites, for they disfigure their faces that their fasting may be seen by men. Truly, I say to you, they have their reward. But when you fast, anoint your head and wash your face, that your fasting may not be seen by men but by your Father

who is in secret; and your Father who sees in secret will reward you. (Matthew 6:16-18)

Before one can deal adequately with Jesus' approach to fasting one must consult Mark 2:18-22 (cf. Matthew 9:14-17 and Luke 5:33-39). Regarding the passage in hand, the attitude of Jesus toward fasting was that already displayed in his treatment of almsgiving and prayer: one who exhibited his personal piety received his reward in popular admiration, and nothing more. No external sign of fasting was necessary, for God needed no such notification of intention. For Jesus, fasting should be private, personal and secretive to be effective.

What does this reveal of Jesus' own faith and practice? Here is where Mark 2:18-22 and its parallels contribute to the understanding of Jesus' own approach to fasting. In the passage quoted above, one would get the impression that he approved and possibly practiced fasting. His only criticism was that of outward show; he feared that the approval of men might be the only motivation and reward of the religious practice of fasting. In Mark 2:18-22, however, he appears to find no place for fasting as a common practice in his gospel. Jesus did not forbid fasting, but he definitely refused to authorize or to sanction it in contemporary practice. He evidently permitted it when it was a matter of self-discipline, at any time the individual chose. The practice must not be continued among his followers simply for its own sake, or as a religious regulation, or at stated times. We do not have any clear statement of Jesus' observing a statutory fast, or even participating in a fast of any kind. He did often go hungry, as is evidenced by the report of his wilderness sojourn (cf. Matthew 4:2-3 and Luke 4:2-3). Evidently Jesus regarded fasting as incapable of meeting the spiritual and moral needs of men.

(25) Do not lay up for yourselves treasures on earth, where moth and rust consume and where thieves break in and steal, but lay up for yourselves treasures in heaven, where neither

moth nor rust consumes and where thieves do not break in and steal. For where your treasure is, there will your heart be also. (Matthew 6:19-21)

This passage reveals Jesus' concept of the material world. The thought expressed here is that hoarding up material goods was due to the age-old quest for security; if man could only possess all the things he needed, then his anxieties regarding the future would be dispersed. Yet Jesus pointed out, with deep insight and wisdom, that not only did such an aggregation of material needs fail to rid one of insecurity, but it increased the anxiety regarding the future. Material goods are a source of anxiety, fear and insecurity, as Jesus indicated, for there are the matters of protection and deterioration involved, as well as selfish pride in them for their beauty, sentimental connections and antiquity value.

Jesus, on the basis of his own experience with material goods, would rather cherish the intangibles of life, such as courage, love, integrity and character. These cannot be attacked and destroyed by physical methods and forces. Once before (Q, Luke 12:4-7; cf. Matthew 10:28-31), we met up with this same concept of things. Thus we see the Hellenistic influences of Galilee playing upon his thought. We do not have here the Hebrew mind that considered flesh and spirit as one; rather, we have the Hellenistic concept of the temporal flesh and the immortal spirit of man assumed in this teaching. Jesus placed his faith in the indestructible nature of man's soul over against the transient, suffering human body. Jesus would rather refine this indestructible incorporeal reality of man than to be overly concerned with the comforts of decaying corporeality, which served only as a "body" or "channel of expression" for the human soul.

(26) Enter by the narrow gate; for the gate is wide and the way is easy, that leads to destruction, and those who enter by it are many. For the gate is narrow and the way is hard, that leads to life, and those who find it are few. (Matthew 7:13-14)

The Faith He Shared

Every great teacher has sought to indicate the choice of ways and means as well as objectives and ends. Parallels for these words of Jesus can be found in Jewish Scriptures and literature, and in Classical writings.

The idea which Jesus propounded is age-old: Vice is always more attractive than virtue. "The way" is always broad and spacious despite the crowds who flock to its concourse: "the line of least resistance." Many are attracted to it; the great multitudes flock to its ease, but such a wide-open road leads only to destruction. The way that leads to the ultimate goal of God's intent for man, namely the rich, full and satisfying life of righteousness, is portrayed as narrow and unattractive, full of obstacles, bruises and suffering, often with death, violent death. The narrow way is the way of self-denial and self-sacrifice. Only when a man stands firm with resolute convictions and a dogged determination does he slowly plod his way to the "celestial city" of eternal life and of the world to come.

> (27) The kingdom of heaven is like treasure hidden in a field, which a man found and covered up; then in his joy he goes and sells all that he has and buys that field.
> Again, the kingdom of heaven is like a merchant in search of fine pearls, who, on finding one pearl of great value, went and sold all that he had and bought it. (Matthew 13:44–46)

Here are two parables which Matthew has placed together; the messages are identical: the man who discovers the true nature of life (as indicated by Jesus in his life and teachings) will spare no effort, and will consider no sacrifice too great, to attain to it. This is the high estimation which Jesus placed upon eternal life. When man saw what Jesus saw, that the Kingdom of God is priceless and of more value than physical life itself, he would willingly part with all his savings for that one "pearl of great price."

Nothing is indicated regarding the morals involved in the

two stories; that is to say, no attention was paid by Jesus as to the source of the hidden treasure, its rightful ownership or the ethical practices related here concerning the reburying of the discovered treasure until more significant individuals were in possession of the land. The second parable is not open to criticism; a better example had been found.

Jesus said that if men feverishly worked themselves to "death" for a mere pittance of material goods which are predestined to extinction, how much more sensible and worth while would it be for men to strive for those eternal intangibles, personal character, social concern and basic righteousness, which never disappear.

> (28) If your brother sins against you, go and tell him his fault, between you and him alone. If he listens to you, you have gained your brother. But if he does not listen, take one or two others along with you, that every word may be confirmed by the evidence of two or three witnesses. If he refuses to listen to them, tell it to the church; and if he refuses to listen even to the church, let him be to you as a Gentile and a tax collector. Truly, I say to you, whatever you bind on earth shall be bound in heaven, and whatever you loose on earth shall be loosed in heaven. Again I say to you, if two of you agree on earth about anything they ask, it will be done for them by my Father in heaven. For where two or three are gathered in my name, there am I in the midst of them. (Matthew 18:15–20)

This passage raises a very pertinent question: Is this saying in its present form direct from Jesus? Or is it some utterance of his which has been fashioned rather thoroughly into a rule dealing with matters in the Church at the time M was written down?

The teaching which is propounded here is this: the person who knows of an offense between himself and another is to make every effort to right the wrong, release the tension, restore confidence and make a friendship blossom. But if these attempts

The Faith He Shared

fail? Then witnesses are to be brought in and the problem stated before them. If the offender fails to repent, then the one offended is to see that the difficulty is publicized in the church. If all these steps fail, then the offender is to be considered as no longer a member of the church. The purpose of these steps appears to be to bring the offender to repentance.

Jesus saw that all tensions and antagonisms between persons were matters of misunderstanding or selfishness. He pleaded for God's grace to abound in human hearts. He asked for one of the offenders to "extend the olive branch" of peace to the other; he trusted human nature to respond to love, forgiveness and compassion. But if for some reason the offender failed to soften his heart in the situation, then another principle was to be applied: Christian social pressure. Jesus, however, believed that the true child of God will act like God in extending the friendly spirit and in being willing to do the unexpected and undeserved "good deed" for the reconciliation of the other.

(29) The disciples said to him, "If such is the case of a man with his wife, it is not expedient to marry." But he said to them, "Not all men can receive this precept, but only those to whom it is given. For there are eunuchs who have been so from birth, and there are eunuchs who have been made eunuchs by men, and there are eunuchs who have made themselves eunuchs for the sake of the kingdom of heaven. He who is able to receive this, let him receive it." (Matthew 19:10–12)

Jesus had just spoken of marriage (cf. Matthew 19:3–9) and had stripped the husband of all easy reasons for divorce. God's intention for male and female was to be found in continence of sex life not only to the gratification of the sexual urges but in fulfillment of sincere love and respect for each other's personalities.

Verse 10 makes the interpretation of this passage difficult. If we take it as the continuation of the previous passage, then what the disciples were saying was this: Why marry at all? But Jesus believed in marriage, the divinely intended means of controlling the reproductive urge in the nature of man. Yet he appeared to acknowledge in the saying three kinds of celibates: those born so, those who allowed themselves to be castrated by their own hands or others, and those who in their zeal for the spiritual life find no "desire" for sexual intercourse, and therefore have no cause for marriage. In specific cases and under certain circumstances, Jesus believed God would approve such celibacy, for the sake of the cause.

(30) But you are not to be called rabbi, for you have one teacher, and you are all brethren. And call no man your father on earth, for you have one Father, who is in heaven. Neither be called masters, for you have one master, the Christ. He who is greatest among you shall be your servant; whoever exalts himself will be humbled, and whoever humbles himself will be exalted. (Matthew 23:8-12)

Jesus perceived a community devoid of distinctions founded amid contemporary Judaism. Titles were dangerous, because they so easily produced what is known as spiritual pride. What Jesus sought to eradicate from the new community was not the desire to show reverence and respect for other human beings but rather the desire to have others respect one's self.

Furthermore, this passage indicates that Jesus sought to undercut the authority of men over their fellow men. There was to be known only one authority in personal and social living, and that was the authority of the Father-God, in whom and by whom we were graciously granted life.

Thus we add further evidence to Jesus' concepts of God and man and their proper regard for each other. For Jesus, God was the Father-God who created all things and, as Creator, the final authority in regard to the intentions of his creations. Thus God was the final judge of man's motives, actions and attitudes. Man, on the other hand, was neither to acknowledge any authority over himself except God, nor to seek self-aggrandizement over his fellows as brethren under the jurisdiction of a fatherly God.

On another occasion, recorded in Mark 11:27–33 (and parallels), during the last week of Jesus' life we see this same article of faith expounded. In replying to the Sanhedrin's question with a question regarding the authority by which John the Baptist operated, Jesus indicated very pointedly that he was of the mind that both he and John had been authorized to minister by God Himself, and that no authorization of the Sanhedrin was necessary. They, in turn, had ignored John, and now were questioning Jesus' actions.

From "Mark"

(31) And they sent to him some of the Pharisees and some of the Herodians, to entrap him in his talk. And they came and said to him, "Teacher, we know that you are true, and care for no man; for you do not regard the position of men, but truly teach the way of God. Is it lawful to pay taxes to Caesar, or not? Should we pay them, or should we not?" But knowing their hypocrisy, he said to them, "Why put me to the test? Bring me a coin, and let me look at it." And they brought one. And he said to them, "Whose likeness and inscription is this?" They said to him, "Caesar's." Jesus said to them, "Render to Caesar the things that are Caesar's, and to God the things that are God's." And they were amazed at him. (Mark 12:13–17; cf. Matthew 22:15–22, Luke 20:20–27)

We are granted the opportunity once again of seeing Jesus' concept of authority. In this instance, however, it is not a matter of authorization but of citizenship. What responsibility does the citizen owe to his community?

Confronted with a two-pronged question, like the one he thrust at the same Sanhedrin regarding the authority by which

John baptized, Jesus declared his convictions: "Render to Caesar the things that are Caesar's, and to God the things that are God's" (Mark 12:17). To have singled out Caesar or God not only would have endangered Jesus' life and ministry but would have been false to his own concept of man's station in life. Here we catch a further glimpse of Jesus' concept of man: Man was a creature of God, yet he was made in God's image, which to Jesus implied sonship. As sons of God, men were citizens of two realms: that of the human and that of the divine. In each capacity there were responsibilities: to Caesar (representing community responsibility) man owed "tribute," that material, spiritual or moral support which was his share in the execution of group benefits; to God (representing heavenly responsibility) man owed "tribute," that material, spirit and moral support which again was his share in the maintenance of spiritual benefits.

Much arguing has taken place over this specific verse (Mark 12:17) at the point where one must determine the boundary line between temporal and eternal jurisdiction. Where does Caesar's authority over the bodies, minds and souls of men stop and God's authority begin? Jesus' clever answer at a psychological moment has not been very satisfying or clarifying for those of his followers who would seek to walk "in his steps."

(32) And Sadducees came to him, who say that there is no resurrection; and they asked him a question, saying, "Teacher, Moses wrote for us that if a man's brother dies and leaves a wife, but leaves no child, the man must take the wife, and raise up children for his brother. There were seven brothers; the first took a wife, and when he died he left no children; and the second took her, and died, leaving no children; and the third likewise; and the seven left no children. Last of all the woman also died. In the resurrection whose wife will she be? For the seven had her as wife."

Jesus said to them, "Is not this why you are wrong, that

The Faith He Shared

you know neither the scriptures nor the power of God? For when they rise from the dead, they neither marry nor are given in marriage, but are like angels in heaven. And as for the dead being raised, have you not read in the book of Moses, in the passage about the bush, how God said to him, 'I am the God of Abraham, and the God of Isaac, and the God of Jacob'? He is not God of the dead, but of the living; you are quite wrong." (Mark 12:18–27; cf. Matthew 22:23–33 and Luke 20:27–38)

This passage gives one an opportunity to observe Jesus' ideas regarding the afterlife. The interesting, yet hypothetical, case of seven brothers and one wife was presented rather scornfully by the Sadducees, who were noted for their religious conservatism. Accepting the Torah as the only canon of divine authority, the Sadducees refused to accept some later doctrines of Judaism, held by the Pharisees, such as beliefs in resurrection and in angels.

Jesus challenged the Sadducees' disbelief in the future life with the two reasons that he believed had caused this lack of faith. First Jesus said the Sadducees failed to realize the power of God; for Jesus, it was within the power and purpose of God to grant immortality to the human soul. Secondly, Jesus told the Sadducees that they were ignorant of those very Scriptures to which they clung so tenaciously. He then propounded this argument: When Yahweh called Moses at the time of the burning bush, Moses asked the "voice" who he was. The reply was not only the revelation of the Divine Name but that of His identity as the God of Abraham, Isaac and Jacob. Now, since in common Jewish faith God was always the God of the living and not of the dead, and since the patriarchs had died centuries before Yahweh spoke to Moses at the burning bush, it was clear to Jesus and it should have been clear to the Sadducees that, although the bodies of the patriarchs lay in well-marked graves, yet they must be alive and with Yahweh. This was Jesus' way of defending his faith in the immortality of the human souls before these disbelieving Sadducees. This has a tinge of Hellenistic thought about it, for it must be recalled that the Jews thought only in the total person.

There is also a further aspect of his belief revealed in this passage. Jesus dismissed the matrimonial aspect of the question rather contemptuously by commenting about not marrying in heaven but remaining as the angels. Jesus' comment on this absence of marriage in the afterlife is most pertinent to our discussion here; for not only did Jesus indicate thereby his belief in resurrection (or immortality) but he revealed his belief about sex. Sex was something reserved for the procreation of physical bodies, and nothing more. It had nothing to do with spiritual living after physical death, nor did it have anything to do with the procreation of human souls. In other words, it would appear that Jesus believed that human souls were created afresh by God; they were immortal thereafter, and were non-sexed in their basic nature. It was on this subtle aspect of Jesus' faith that the Christian support of democracy and socialism was established. All men were equal in the sight of God; such arbitrary matters as age, sex, class, creed, race, language and national loyalty were temporal and earthly. Souls were souls, and the characteristics of human souls have a common identity. The variety of mankind was one of degree and quality, not one of basic substance.

(33) And one of the scribes came up and heard them disputing with one another, and seeing that he answered them well, asked him, "Which commandment is the first of all?" Jesus answered, "The first is, 'Hear, O Israel: The Lord our God, the Lord is one; and you shall love the Lord your God with all your heart, and with all your soul, and with all your mind, and with all your strength.' The second is this, 'You shall love your neighbor as yourself.' There is no other commandment greater than these." And the scribe said to him, "You are right, Teacher; you have truly said that he is one, and there is no other but he; and to love him with all the heart, and with all the understanding, and with all the

strength, and to love one's neighbor as oneself, is much more than all whole burnt offerings and sacrifices." And when Jesus saw that he answered wisely, he said to him, "You are not far from the kingdom of God." And after that no one dared to ask him any question. (Mark 12:28-34; cf. Matthew 22:34-40, Luke 10:25-28, 20:39-40)

In this great and familiar passage we can take note of Jesus' only demands upon others: perhaps one should say that these are God's demands upon his children. Jesus was simply voicing the basic divine law, and no other commandments were necessary if these were obeyed. They were the foundation stones of righteousness and peace among men. These were tantamount to survival. To disobey was to be "lost," to face annihilation spiritually as well as mentally, and ofttimes physically. To obey them was to fulfill, as by-products, the Law and the Prophets. The Ten Commandments became unnecessary for those who obeyed these Two Commandments; for those who truly loved God and their neighbor would follow, as night the day, the precepts contained in the Decalogue. To love one's neighbor as oneself made impossible those deeds which called forth restraining legislation. Warnings against theft and murder became meaningless, for the inclinations of human hearts to do such deeds would be lacking. The Divine Will working itself out in individual lives finds true expression in human righteousness. Harmony within the souls of men and among men of all types came, not through the disciples of duty, fear or promised reward, but through the manifesting of a new spirit born of such love of God and man as Jesus was talking about. Jesus had put his finger upon the secret of mature living: man's devotion, love and loyalty to God as Father would find expression in brotherly concern and helpfulness in the everyday living in community.

(34) And as Jesus taught in the temple, he said, "How can the scribes say that the Christ is the son of David? David himself, inspired by the Holy Spirit, declared,

> 'The Lord said to my Lord,
> Sit at my right hand,
> till I put thy enemies under thy feet.'

David himself calls him Lord; so how is he his son?" And the great throng heard him gladly. (Mark 12:35-37; cf. Matthew 22:44-46, Luke 20:41-44)

It is not quite clear just what Jesus was seeking to point out in this passage. Some have believed that Jesus was attacking the popular notions of the Messiah, that such a one *must* be of the line of David. If this be true, can it be that Jesus felt that he *was* the Messiah yet knew that he was *not* of Davidic descent? This would be most interesting and disturbing. Paul, "Matthew," and Luke all declare, however, that Jesus *was* of Davidic descent. Therefore, what other point was Jesus seeking to make? This leads to a more orthodox position: Jesus was saying that in David's very declaration of the Messiah being his Lord, he was indicating a divine descent, a divine origin for the Messiah, despite his earthly lineage from David's line.

Jesus appears to have so regarded the words received from the voice out of heaven: "Thou art my son, my beloved; with thee am I well pleased." Here we see Jesus' belief in himself. This belief was not born of self-esteem and pride, as has been said, but of an experience wherein he felt chosen, selected and anointed. It was not of his own free choice; God had acted, and who could refuse God? Thus he accepted the honor but, more so, the responsibility and gave his very life in personal integrity to it. Duty (i.e., under compulsion) had no part in Jesus' life and motives. Nothing was done or said because Jesus felt he had to. His actions and words were what they were because they were the genuine expression of true devotion and of an indwelling spirit, an inclination of soul that characterized him through constant fellowship and love for his God and his fellow men. Cheerfully he accepted his position, divinely bestowed, and lived it out naturally and normally to its conclusion in frightful agony but inner joyfulness.

The Faith He Shared

In these selections of Jesus' teaching we see the faith of Jesus as he sought to formalize it for public consumption. At no time did he attempt to systematize or dogmatize his beliefs. Yet modern man would like to see them, handle them and study them for the understanding, restoration and regeneration of his own soul. This will be our concluding task as we seek to analyze his faith in doctrinal statements and in fundamental principles.

CHAPTER VII

THE FAITH THAT WAS IN HIM

One significant fact that comes to the surface whenever anyone meditates upon the life of Jesus is this: no mention is ever made by Jesus of religion as such. Apparently Jesus was primarily concerned with man's relationship to God and to his fellow men all in a single context. Jesus thought that the key to man's quality of character and to peaceful interpersonal relationships was to be found in the wholeness of the divine-human relationship. Life always had religious meaning and significance, because man forever lived in the atmosphere of God's presence. The daily life and activities of man were to be interpreted, judged and rewarded according to universal values established by God Himself.

Jesus appears to be in the true Judaic prophetic tradition when he refused to regard spiritual life as a specialized aspect apart from the total experience of life. He struggled desperately against institutionalized religion, wherein religion became confined to specific occasions, places, seasons and rituals. Jesus' condensation of the Law into love of God and love of one's neighbors reveals his concept of religion as one of vital daily living guided by the divine-human relationships of life.

We see Jesus, therefore, placing emphasis upon ethical manifestations and their motivations in attitudes and purposes (Matthew 7:21, 12:33; cf. John 7:17 and Matthew 11:4–6). He appears most desirous of making clear where the keys to life were to be found. The secret of righteous living was to be found in the nature and quality of the inner being of man. Only as this inner being of each individual became increasingly God-like in character and motivations would there be fulfillment and maturity for the individual, and fellowship and concord among mankind. Attempting to embody the ethical attributes of these desired ends without first discovering and setting aright the inner resources upon which these attributes depend would only result in tragedy, as many an average Christian in each generation can testify. Nowhere does Jesus appear to have stated in clear-cut abstract terms the fundamental principles, attitudes and values which a person *must* possess before he can manifest a moral and radiant life worthy of sonship to God and brotherhood to his fellow men. If Jesus ever did so enunciate them, his disciples and recorders completely missed their significance, for the records certainly show no evidence of his teaching specific precepts like the Ten Commandments or a Christian creed which could be memorized and assimilated or intellectually affirmed. Jesus was more profound than that. He knew that he was dealing with intangibles, and he sought to leave them in that state by wise use of parables and pithy sayings that only hint at the truths he was seeking to indicate. Embedded in the teachings that have come down to us through the understanding and enunciation of others, we can still discern certain basic concepts of motivating factors which Jesus had discovered in his own analysis of his life and actions. The teachings were his attempt to present these profoundly significant factors in human experience in terms which his humble contemporaries could understand. He sought to indicate to his followers the way of fulfillment, the means to godlikeness, often referred to as "the way of salvation." What he taught was a shared faith and experience. This was his task as he saw it; this was his mission in life.

A comprehensive investigation as well as a complete understanding of the faith of Jesus is impossible. Circumstances beyond our control hinder anyone at this point in history from adequately expressing for the modern mind Jesus' fundamental doctrines, much less his vibrant and vigorous faith. Yet aspects of that faith appear to exude from certain basic assumptions and beliefs which, as faith, result in ethical by-products. These ethical manifestations are emphasized vigorously in Jesus' teaching.

So much has been assumed or left unsaid by Jesus' recorders; that which the various accounts gives us is merely the selected material of preachers, teachers and writers whose purposes were other than ours. Yet, however frustrating our research may be, certain valid conclusions can be stated in the light of the information and impressions made by the investigations recorded in previous chapters.

Each chapter of this work has spoken for itself, with no summary conclusions; the reader has been counted upon to recognize and gather up the facts and factors involved in a study of the faith of Jesus. Now the time has come when a succinct statement of some of those basic beliefs of Jesus is called for.

God

The key to one's understanding of Jesus' life and thought is to be found in his concept and experience of God. In present-day terms, the integration of Jesus' life centered in God: God was the focal point of his commitment; God's Will was the focal drive of his life; God's compassion for mankind was the dominant spirit of his life; God's mind was the vantage point from which Jesus looked upon life. It is no wonder, then, that his earliest disciples came to realize in a rather uncanny way that they were fellowshipping with God all the while. In Jesus they saw God; they felt God's concern and spirit; they sensed divine authority. In reality, it was not God but the Good Life to which they were responding. God was other than Jesus, just as Jesus was other than they. Only when we catch glimpses of Jesus' God in thought and experience will we even begin to comprehend Jesus or the good life he embodied.

Even before Jesus was considerably aware of God's presence, he had been taught by faithful parents and neighborhood rabbis that there was but one God, the Father of His chosen people,

The Faith That Was in Him

Israel. Jesus never heard a discussion on the question of the existence of God; that was a basic, inherent assumption on the part of everyone. Whether or not God *was* never entered the mind of a Jew. God was, He is, He always will be! The fact of one God, for the Jew, was a proud doctrine of the faith into which Jesus was born. Non-Jews might argue over the number and existence of their various gods and goddesses, but for Jesus and the Jews there was but one God, who was the Creator of all things, and the Father of His chosen people.

The omniscience and omnipotence of God appear to have been assumed by Jesus. Like God's existence, His "all-power" and "all-knowing" are simply taken for granted. Along with God's omnipresence, these were the unquestionably assumed attributes of God as the Jews naturally conceived Him. Jesus certainly accepted them, for did he not say something about "every sparrow that falls" (Matthew 10:29)? He recognized the power of God and did not allow for its arbitrary use, where the existent laws of God were known to man and relied upon by man.

The God whom Jesus knew was that very God who had made Himself known to the patriarchs of the nation: Abraham, Isaac, Jacob and Joseph. He was the very God who spoke to Moses through the burning bush and upon the holy mount of the Torah. The God of Jesus was the God of the Jewish nation, known by his sacred name, Yahweh. He was the God of history, who revealed His Will in the destiny of men and nations. His word had been uttered in the volcanic voice on Mount Sinai, in the proclamations and exhortations of the Prophets, and in the quiet but powerful voice of the written word of Holy Writ. As Jesus said on at least one important occasion, God hath spoken: "They have Moses and the prophets; let them hear them" (Luke 16:29).

For Jesus, knowledge of God was not exclusively intellectual in nature. There was also one's experience of God. Just how early in human existence one can become aware of other persons, and especially of metaphysical persons, is still a moot question. Some believe the human infant, that little bundle of responses, begins immediately to respond to external stimuli, both things and persons. Long before a child can speak, certainly before he can give intellectual expression to his awarenesses, he responds to interpersonal emanations. From childhood Jesus worshipped God; the holy Temple in distant Jerusalem became for Jesus his Father's house (Luke 2:49). The devotional atmosphere of a devout household also played its part. Undoubtedly there are those who would like to believe that from the very beginning Jesus' spiritual awareness surpassed normal human experience. Yet it is more probable that God in His infinite wisdom trusted His divinely initiated laws of growth and development until they held full sway. Therefore Mary and Joseph are due some long-overdue praise for their guidance and fellowship with a most precocious and spiritually sensitive child.

For Jesus, God appears to have always been a Person with whom one could have actual intimate fellowship. Such experiential awareness of God made it impossible for Jesus ever to think of God as a vague first cause, an elemental force in the universe or any other abstract principle. For Jesus, God was a Person with whom one could have fellowship and mutual understanding. The intriguing aspect of Jesus' concept of a personal God is found in his designation *Abba*. *Abba* is the Aramaic for the intimate father, or, as we would say, "daddy." This would indicate that Jesus accepted the idea that God was the Father of Israel. To this he added the ingredients of a happy home life wherein Joseph was a real daddy to the boy. Perhaps it was upon the death of Joseph that the early-adolescent Jesus transferred his filial piety to the Heavenly Father of his nation, and his Heavenly Father gained stature and significance in his life.

Jesus' approaches to his Heavenly Father took the form of prayer periods and moments apart from the noise and confusion of busy thoroughfares. In the quiet of some garden spot, or upon some lonely hill, away from civilization were his traditional abiding places for conscious fellowship and communication with his *Abba*.

In true Judaic fashion, the Father-God was always regarded

as someone other than the one praying. The immanence of God, or the mystical union with the Father which a Johannine treatment later gave to the Jesus-God relationship, does not appear in any of the earlier tradition found in the first three Gospels. If the fourth Gospel is recording a true statement of Jesus, then in the light of other evidence we are compelled to interpret the saying "I and the Father are one" (John 10:30) in this fashion: "I and the Father are of one mind and heart, for I have willed to do His Will," and not "I and the Father are one in substance, and therefore He is immanent in me." Jesus always regarded God as one other than himself. No matter how much godlikeness Jesus revealed in his thought and actions, he never regarded himself as God, or as in mystical union with God in any immanental way. He appears to prefer to think of himself as God's son rather than by any other messianic title, such as the Son of Man or the Messiah. The Father-God is always, in Jesus' thinking, one to whom one can turn in prayer for immediate help and strength. God is ever near but never immanent.

Thus we see that Jesus' concept of God, built upon personal experience, was a healthy-minded, well-rounded idea and reality of Deity. For Jesus, God's mind was Truth; His concepts were best; His attitudes were most satisfying. When one came truly "to think God's thoughts after Him," one gained proper perspective; he saw with profound insight into the meaning and purpose of life, with all its joys and sorrows, its health and pain, its good and evil. Thus, for Jesus, God's mind was Truth.

For Jesus, God's Will was Destiny. Man was given an independent will which has tempted man to covet God's power and initiative. Yet when man learns to will the Will of God, there is an unfolding goodness and happiness which exceeds the deepest longings of the human soul. This is no slave-despot relationship, nor is it a disrespect for human willfulness. Rather, this is the human being willing his best—willing to ascend to heights of wisdom and service with the greatest ease and health in body, mind and soul.

Finally, for Jesus, God's spirit was Love, and this Love was the law of life. He pointed up this aspect of his faith in his summary of the Law in two commandments: love God, love neighbor as you love yourself. Only through the sincere and genuine experience and emanation of Love does one realize the good life, personally and socially. When Love rules and characterizes a person's life, there is truly a deep-seated satisfaction within a man. When Love rules and characterizes a person's relationships to his family, neighbors and strangers, there is a quick response, and brotherhood is established. Respect, compassion, and patience characterize one's relationship with strangers and enemies. Through his intimate association with such a God, Jesus came to be characterized by the selfsame attributes and therefore was mistakenly analyzed as the incarnation or literal embodiment of the Godhead. It would appear to be the intent of God to encompass His children with His Mind, Will, and Spirit. Then people will come to recognize the rightness, goodness and compassion of God so as to cause them to seek attunement to His person, thereby manifesting in their own lives His intended qualities of sonship.

The World

Jesus appears to have accepted and assumed popular Jewish ideas concerning the universe. There was no thought of galaxies of universes; the cosmos in which man found himself living on the planet Earth was the only known one. In fact, the stationary earth was the center around or over which the sun, the moon and the movable stars were maneuvered. The earth had been created by God, who had created everything else men knew about.

There appears to have been a consensus of opinion regarded as factual in this connection. The characteristics of the world were obvious to all who had eyes to see: a half-globe dome of blue firmament encased earth; part of the earth was submerged below water, and part of it was forced heavenward to form hills and mountains. Upon this relatively flat earth men dwelt, as did all the birds, beasts and fish about which men knew. There were also plants, shrubs and trees of many kinds, and both barren and fertile soil. But the man, the family, the tribe who was in possession, chiefly by being settled upon land where good crops were forthcoming, was fortunate indeed.

Below the good earth the only sure thing was "the waters under the earth," which were regarded as the sources of the rivers, wells, fountains and springs. Such sources of life-giving water protected from the beastly heat of the semi-tropical atmosphere in which they lived were among the blessings of God. Yet somewhere below these waters, men believed, was a Sheol, a Hades, a nether region inhabited by departed spirits of dead human beings; in "the bowels of the earth" abode the souls of all the dead.

The sun, moon and moving stars were believed to be under God's angelic control, and maneuvered within the firmament space. Replacing the traditional Greek gods and the concepts that Greek mythology used to explain and describe these phenomena, the Jews maintained that Yahweh was in complete control with angelic hosts doing His bidding in the movements of sun, moon and stars, of rain, snow and other atmospheric phenomena such as clouds and unpredictable winds, especially the sirocco. In this common belief Jesus shared; for did he not say: "The wind bloweth where it wills" (John 3:8) or, again, "What went ye out into the wilderness to behold? A reed shaken with the wind?" (Matthew 11:7.)

Yet in keeping with Hellenistic thought, the Jews, using Jewish terminology and looking from a Judaistic vantage point, also believed in the seven-story heaven above the firmament, each inhabited by angelic or demonic beings whose tasks varied according to divine allocation of duties. Those angels in the first heaven above the firmament, for example, were responsible for the natural phenomena of rain, snow, the sun, the moon and clouds. It was the fourth heaven—or was it the fifth?—in which Satan and his "forces" made his celestial habitation. Into the third heaven living human souls could mount godward for judgment and redemption, as evidenced by Paul's statement in II Corinthians 12:2. God watched over his creation from the perfect habitation designated "seventh heaven," wherein was the throne of the heavenly oriental potentate in all his majesty. Herein no human soul was ever found worthy to enter—until Jesus' soul was thought and declared to be so worthy.

All this Jesus appears to have accepted and assumed in his talks with the people. Many of his well-remembered sayings give evidence of his utter faith in the world, in its innate goodness, its ability to feed men (if man's selfishness and bigotry did not interfere). Like the country boy he was, Jesus illustrated his profound spiritual and moral insights by the homely observations of youth: there were the birds and their nests, the fox and its hole (Matthew 8:20, Luke 9:58); there were grasses in the fields (Matthew 6:30, Luke 12:28), which God created and continued to maintain. Although Jesus was a carpenter by trade, he knew his farm problems: some seeds cast in traditional fashion fell upon stony soil, some on hard-packed paths, some amidst thorns, while others fell upon good ground and brought forth a harvest (Matthew 13:3–9, Mark 4:3–9 and Luke 8:5–8). He also knew the problems of the fishermen on the Sea of Galilee, for did he not say: "When it is evening, you say, 'It will be fair weather; for the sky is red.' And in the morning, 'It will be stormy today, for the sky is red and threatening'" (Matthew 16:2–3)? And from the rain and the sunshine Jesus gained a symbol for his concept of God's justice and the problem of evil (Matthew 5:45).

In the light of these observations, and in an atmosphere of popular opinions, Jesus sought to call his people to God's providential care. Jesus believed God bestowed his blessings freely. Wherein man has not abused the gift of good earth, and has practiced soil conservation, Jesus believed there would be no lack of the essentials of physical existence. He believed also that these good gifts, so essential to human existence, were intended for all, equally; for those who opposed His will and lived in despicable sin received the blessings of God in equal proportion with the righteous person. He sought to prove this point by his reference to the sun shining upon the evil and the good, and His rain falling with its refreshing coolness on the unjust man as well as the just. God, Jesus believed, stood ever ready to forgive man, if he would but turn from his blindness and see these gracious facts. Thus we see Jesus advocating that man look about himself and note God's care for His creatures.

Man

The quality of a religion can be judged by its concept of man. Next to deity, the most important factor in any religion is its concept of man. This is none the less true of the faith of Jesus; in fact, Jesus' concept of and attitude toward man is one of the unique characteristics not only of his personal faith but of that of his followers.

Once again we must note at the outset that there are certain aspects of Jesus' concept of man that remain unstated assumptions in his mind. Yet in our presentation we shall endeavor to give the total picture: both the inherited aspects and the personalized faith in man.

First of all, Jesus appears to have accepted the basic Jewish concept of the origin of man: he regarded man as a particular creation of God. He does not state how God created man, or how man had developed to his recognizable state in the first Christian century. He appears to have simply placed his faith in the Genesis story as he inherited it, and as it still appears in Scripture. Evidently there was no felt need to discuss the matter, and Jesus did not. He was as simple as that: "So God created man in his own image, in the image of God he created him; male and female he created them" (Genesis 1:27).

For Jesus' Jewish audience, man was conceived as a psychophysical unity. Born a unity of corporeal and noncorporeal substances, man lived a unity and died a unity. The Jew then believed that man remained dead (in some "suspended sleep," biologically unaccountable) until some future resurrection, when he would be raised as "a unity" once more.

In what sense did Jesus believe that man was created in the image of God? Certainly not in the flesh or material sense. Rather, Jesus appears to have had a tinge of the Hellenistic concept of man at this point; he accepted the fact that man by nature was a strange mixture of the corporeal and the noncorporeal elements of life. The Jew, as it would appear, could not disembody the spirit from the material body through which the spirit gained expression. To the Jew, there was always a body present where being was. This Jesus may have accepted from his Jewish intellectual inheritance and atmosphere, yet it is equally clear that Jesus placed more and more emphasis upon the spiritual aspect of man's nature. For Jesus, it was the inner man that counted most (cf. Matthew 15:17–18); it was with the image of God that Jesus was most concerned. He sought to make these separate images true reflections of God as he was.

Thus Jesus saw man as the crown and summit of God's creative power and purpose. Whatever interfered with the realization of these highest potentialities in human character met with the determined resistance of Jesus. Whatever awakened and encouraged those factors that would bring to fruition the divine qualities of character which the phrase "the image of God" sought to indicate met the enthusiastic support of Jesus. Herein we see a more positive, hopeful and sane concept of man than we discover in Paul and the later Church.

Sin

From both Hebrew and Greek the word for "sin" could be translated as "a missing of the mark." Speaking ethically, therefore, for some the mark would be the accepted mores of a culture; for others the mark would be obedience to a set of rules or laws. Yet the Jew never lost sight of what he considered "a revealed truth," that God created man in His own image. Thus for the Jew the mark was this image of God. Sin became that which deflected the soul of man from reflecting this likeness of God.

Priest and prophet of Judaism had joined forces to state that salvation came through doing the Will of God. The Will of God had been enunciated in the Torah. Therefore, whenever an individual failed to keep Torah, he sinned and fell under condemnation. The presence of Torah kept all Jews conscious of their sin and degradation. Thus, through the years various means of redemption were worked out in cultic practices, such as various tributes, fasts and sacrifices. This only increased the power of the priests over the people, and prophetic insights were overwhelmed and almost lost from sight.

Then John the Baptist and Jesus came and sought to restate and re-establish the prophetic norm. The emphasis was laid upon the moral and the spiritual contradistinction to the ceremonial and the legal. Therefore we should note with care how Jesus indicated the point of sin—or, should we say, the seat of sin? For Jesus the key lay at the point of human inclination and motivation rather than in outer actions. We hear him say: "It was said of old time . . . but I say unto you . . ." Jesus was concerned with God's underlying intent or moral principle in a given law.

The important point for Jesus in the question of "sin" was the volitional attitude, not the actual commitment. In this regard we see that there was a matter of definite relativity involved —an attitude taken, not a standard attained. Sins were the product of maladjustments, of wrong inclinations, evil intentions and bad motives. Righteous living, in turn, was the fruit of proper adjustment to life, of good intentions, righteous inclinations and correct motives. Thus we see that the essential element was the inner quality of the human soul (cf. Mark 7:1–23). When that inner quality was not up to par man failed to express those attributes of a son of God, made in His image. When that inner quality was refined into an ever-increasing godlikeness, man's true maturation was being achieved. "Become ye mature as your

Father is mature" was Jesus' hope, dream and expectation for himself and every child of God.

A further word needs to be said. It would appear that Jesus' concept of sin allowed for considerable adjustment. That which was sin for one individual might not be so for another. Perhaps this point can best be illustrated by Jesus' treatment of the rich young ruler: Jesus regarded great possessions as the chief sin for this young man, yet it is clear that it was not his possessions but his attitude and the inclination of his soul toward those possessions that were the seat of his sin. In other words, riches for one person may not be sinful for him, but for this particular young man they were a sin that separated him from God and his rightful heritage of sonship to God. Each case has to be judged on its own merits; no set of rules or general standard can be applied to each individual.

Sin, therefore, in the faith of Jesus, may be defined as that combination of inner motives and inclinations which affect man's attitudes and actions and result in failure to mirror the Godhead. Anything which causes deflection in the image of God is sin.

The Means of Salvation

Perhaps this section does not qualify for a statement of doctrine, but its inclusion in this chapter is imperative. In true prophetic spirit Jesus called upon mankind to repent (Matthew 3:2). In this we note that for Jesus the means to salvation open with an earnest summons to reconsider life and its meaning. Repentance for Jesus, therefore, was not simply a matter of remorse over past sins but exactly what the word connotes, a matter of repentance, *repenser,* rethinking. For only as man can comprehend God's intent for his life can he desire that which is good, true and beautiful.

Jesus knew that man was very much aware of his "lostness" and sin. He also believed that man could "become perfect." But

The Faith That Was in Him

what was this "perfectness"? No better illustration can be found than that of the Greek word *sodzo*, a word that, as found in the New Testament, has been given two different English translations. Sometimes (Mark 10:26) *sodzo* has been given the theological and traditional linguistic equivalent in English "saved," but elsewhere (Mark 3:5, 5:34) *sodzo* is out of the theological context and therefore is transliterated into English by the phrase "made whole." Therefore we can see that in Jesus' day (and we may assume thereby in his *thought*) "to be saved" meant "to be made whole" or, more clearly, "to be restored to God's intended normality." Thus salvation is that state of human life (social and individual) wherein God's image is fulfilled and God's Kingdom comes on earth as it presumably is in heaven. That which is normal to men is really abnormal; and salvation, usually regarded as something supernormal (or supernatural), is in divine reality "the normal" as God envisioned and intended it. Only by man's immaturity, ignorance or selfish willfulness has God been thwarted and sin entered the experience of men. But what is sought at this juncture of our study of Jesus' doctrines is the *means* from sin to salvation. How did Jesus believe a man "became saved" spiritually?

The first step after repentance appears to be a matter of spiritual "attunement," if we may so describe it. Through personal and public worship and prayer, Jesus believed, one entered into such communion of spirit that something akin to the tuning process of musical instruments took place. As the instrument approximated the tuning fork, so the soul of the communicant became attuned to God's spirit. It was in a real sense a matter of sympathetic approximation of God's spirit. Through ever-increasing frequence of spiritual fellowship and communion, something of God's love and friendliness, rightness and justice, "rubbed off" upon the worshipper. This was the beginning of one's journey toward salvation and the full life.

Almost contemporaneously there took place a meeting and fellowshipping of minds—so Jesus thought would appear—when man was "feeling his way" into those great insights and matters of wisdom present in the mind of God. Again one may say it was a process of attunement wherein man thought God's thoughts after Him until that glorious day when man has become so attuned that he is at one in thought with God, that he almost can foreknow what God will think, and in such a moment the "saved" person will respond as God intended. In such a moment divine wisdom will be manifested in the attitudes and judgments of the mature individual, "the saved person."

But the real key to unlocking "the moment of salvation" (which Paul called "justification," John called the moment of "rebirth," and Jesus described as "entrance into the Kingdom of God") was the attunement of wills. Jesus once said: "Whoever does the will of God is my brother, and sister, and mother" (Mark 3:35). In this he put his finger on the key to complete salvation, for only when man voluntarily attunes his own will to that of the Father does the process of reintegration take place. Jesus dramatized this feature of his faith in his own practice, as evidenced in the famous prayer in Gethsemane; there, when his own will was to escape danger, he abandoned all to do the Will of his Heavenly Father. Such abandonment was the experience of volitional attunement. The electrifying result was a Christ-like character manifested by God-like attitudes and conduct.

Actually, the means to salvation as Jesus understood them are best explained as this process of attunement—a process of contemporaneous attunement of man's spirit, mind and will to those of the Father-God. Such attunement results in a true at-one-ment which is true atonement indeed. As the prophets before him (cf. Micah 6:6–8), so now Jesus emphasized the demand of God in terms of resulting ethical attitudes and acts rather than of ceremonial exactitude or legal obedience. God, as Jesus saw it, was more interested in "the set of the sail" of a man's soul than in man's exacting obedience to a prescribed norm. The nature of the resulting life-fulfillment becomes our next concern.

Salvation

In the religion of Jesus the concepts of sin and salvation are intimately connected. Both concepts are likewise closely connected with his concept of man. One of Jesus' deepest convictions was that man had lost contact with God and His Will. In this "lostness" man wandered about in sin, until "he came to himself" and discovered that his hunger was not for fame, wealth, a thrill, or power but for spiritual salvation, personal fulfillment. In his divinely given free will, man had sought to fathom his own potentialities and capabilities and live by them, to no avail.

To this estate of man Jesus addressed himself. Jesus appears to have been more positive in his approach to the problem. He sought to help the individual to recognize his God-given potentialities and then to encourage that individual to step out in faith into that new life. Perhaps no better illustration of this can be had than his dealing with the adulteress brought before him in the Temple one day (John 7:53—8:11). After he had dispersed her persecutors and the curious, he said to her very simply: "Go, and do not sin again" (John 8:11). For Jesus, God demanded only that the sinner, having recognized his sin, have the courage to step out in the faith of a little child seeking to take its first unassisted and unsupported step in the process of learning to walk. In fact, we well know that on another occasion Jesus actually said, "Except ye turn and become as a little child ye cannot enter the kingdom of God" (cf. Mark 10:15).

In this position Jesus was aligned with the prophets rather than with the priests. The transactional element in the redemptive process is practically missing in Jesus' teachings; there are only two questionable allusions to it, in Mark 10:45 (cf. Luke 22:24–29) and Mark 14:22–25. In all the rest of his recorded teachings, nothing appeared to be expected of the sinner beyond remorse except to step forth in faith and live as though he were already saved, and the joy of salvation would be his. There was no thought of sacrificial transaction in this, as there has been in traditional Christian faith ever since the "stumblingblock" of the cross. This absence of a sacrificial transaction in Jesus' concept of salvation is most conspicuous; even the parable of the Prodigal Son leaves out this feature in Jesus' indirect presentation of his concept of redemption. The only atonement is the bitter realization of one's mistake and the practical determination to remedy it. This is obviously the prophetic concept of redemption, as seen in the great passages such as Micah 6:6–8.

Since for Jesus salvation was that *to which* one was redeemed, the question naturally rises: what was the nature of such salvation for him? In simple terms, salvation was the release from the sins that so easily beset man; but more than that, it was the abundant *joie de vivre* which one experienced when all guilt was erased from the soul and old temptations no longer plagued one. Only new temptations to righteous living and the awakened awareness to beauty, truth and goodness thrust one into an exciting and an abundant life. One discovered living in the image of God more satisfying than existing by one's own wits. Salvation was thus the God-intended life of the individual and of human society, with all its eagerness and adventure in the unfolding capabilities and powers of men. As in the life of a child, so in the life of salvation—in every incident, new discovery, exciting experience, mysterious happening and unknown tomorrow—there was joy and adventure with the Father-God as He spiritually guides one along life's way toward fulfillment.

For Jesus, salvation was a Way, a process: "Become ye . . ." One does not jump from the "blackness" of sin to the "whiteness" of bliss, but, rather, is led by God through the various shades of "grayness" and, depending upon the increasing or decreasing amounts of faith in God, grows more like the Father in character, will, conduct and spirit. This would likewise appear to be the Way which Jesus himself traversed, wherein "he increased in wisdom and in stature, and in favor with God and man" (Luke 2:52). As it had been his Way, so it became "the Way"; and he is the proof of its rightness and divine source.

The Faith That Was in Him 161

Since it was an unfolding experience in life, Jesus became increasingly aware of the need for constant nurturing. Those moments in prayer, those periods of synagogue attendance, his consistent attendance at the great religious festivals at the Temple in Jerusalem, are obvious evidences of his deliberate and conscious efforts to refine and develop the quality of his life unto fulfillment. His teachings regarding prayer, almsgiving and fasting likewise point to his own personal "practicing of the Presence." Even Jesus needed to improve and increase his sensitivities of soul to the presence of God. He apparently needed to improve and increase his awareness of the will of God in order that he could attune his own will to that of his Father. Only as he basked in the radiance of God's presence, love and understanding did he believe that he would truly become an "image" of the Father.

The success of his methods and techniques are to be recognized in theological explanations of the later Christian Church wherein they were unable to disentangle Jesus from God. Thereupon the historical Jesus of Nazareth was no longer considered the son of God, or even the incarnation of God, but God Himself made flesh. Yet in like manner he appears to have expected his followers to walk his "Way of salvation" until they, like him, would truly reflect the Father. Even Paul caught this "vision," for he saw Jesus as the "first-born among many brethren" (Romans 8:29) and "the second Adam" (cf. Romans 5), a sort of new *genus* of mankind, made new from having laid hold on those "forces" latent in man's very being "from the beginning." And all those who "learn of Jesus" the way of life would share in the *joie de vivre* found in fellowship with God in the doing of His Will.

What, then, is the nature of the ultimate goal of this "Way"? Toward what kind of finale was the way of salvation leading? Any alert reader can suspect that the simple answer is clear: the end result of this developing or unfolding process is a community of individuals fashioned into "the image of God," living in "heavenly harmony," in filial piety.

Salvation, therefore, in Jesus' mind appears to have had little or at least only indirect connection with the "gifts," occupations and "skills" of individual human beings. Jesus was concerned only with the character and motives of men. Set the inner resources of individuals aright, and the resulting attitudes and actions would take care of themselves. "For as a man thinketh in his heart so is he" (cf. Proverbs 23:7, A.V.). "Thus you will know them by their fruits," Jesus had said (Matthew 7:20). It can be safely assumed that Jesus believed that, once a man was living as an "image of God," then his attitudes and actions would manifest the true character of his being and his "gifts," occupations and "skills" would improve and become more productive.

In the second place, ultimate salvation, in the mind of Jesus, took little if any cognizance of the physical aspects of the individuals involved. Size, shape, race, sex, age seem superfluous considerations in regard to man's spiritual redemption and total maturation. He did say, "But seek first his kingdom and his righteousness, and all these things shall be yours as well" (Matthew 6:33). Herein he is saying that spiritual redemption will correct the physical, mental and emotional disorders of the individual, and in turn will affect that individual's social relationships unto the refinement of societal living, like unto that conceived of as that of heaven.

In a third place, salvation was, in Jesus' thinking, not exclusively an individual matter but was a societal redemption as well. Society cannot be saved except through personal redemption of individuals; and persons cannot be completely saved until the society wherein they live and work is redeemed. The very fact that Jesus continued the social concept of redemption is to be noted in his constant reference to the Kingdom of God. Jesus conceived of it as a real kingdom, a society, which, in Old Testament terms, was the covenant-people, the true Israel, apart from whom there can be *no* personal salvation.

The Kingdom of God

In the messianic enthusiasm of Judaism in Jesus' day there were two key terms: *Messiah* and *the Kingdom of God*. In Jesus' personal ministry and message he rejected the former (and we will later explain why, when we consider his messianic consciousness), and the latter he accepted, though he redefined it and refined it by his personal touch.

The Kingdom of God was the central theme of his ministry. Jesus preached it; he prayed for it; he taught it; he lived it; and he died for it. Some scholars believe that Jesus did not think of the Kingdom as existing before his earthly ministry.

The Kingdom of God was certainly the focal point of his personal religion. As we have seen, Jesus' baptism was his commitment to it in devout allegiance. We have also noted that his so-called "temptation" was the defining of his personal relationship to it, as well as the qualifying of his understanding of its nature. His prayer life centers about his deep concern for its manifestation—best illustrated in these familiar words: "Thy kingdom come, thy will be done" (Matthew 6:10, cf. Luke 11:2c). If Matthew's Gospel record does not deceive us, Jesus accepted the clarion call of John the Baptist as his own: "Repent, for the kingdom of heaven is at hand" (Matthew 3:2,4,17b). Both John and Jesus spoke out of deep personal experiences of sharing in the Kingdom. And his death? For his part in bringing in the kingdom Jesus gave his life in the most heroic act of personal integrity and commitment.

We have just quoted Matthew's recorded word of Jesus in which the phrase appears—"the kingdom of *heaven*." Matthew alone used this phrase. The evidence indicates that Jesus used the rather un-Jewish phrase "the kingdom of God." The fourth Gospel's use of the term "eternal life" in place of "the kingdom of God" seems to have been a Johannine attempt to use an Hellenistic concept for a Jewish one in regard to the reality of a covenant people which underlay both terms. Yet this Johannine expression emphasizes the personal aspect of the matter, to the neglect of the societal part indicated by the very use of the word "kingdom."

The important aspects, as Jesus conceived them, were religious, not political. The reign of God in human hearts and thereby in society as well was the core of the concept. As Jesus understood it, God rules unconquerably in human history. For Jesus, God has an absolute claim upon man.

Perhaps this rather complicated reality of the Kingdom of God may be better understood if these four facets of the Kingdom are presented. Jesus once said: "The kingdom of God is within you" (cf. Luke 17:20); obviously he was not speaking of the "invasion" of some mysterious thing into one's inward part. Rather, he was saying that the *inward quality* of a saved one's life, the fruit of God's Will being willed by that particular individual, constitutes one aspect of the Kingdom of God. The Kingdom has come when His Will is done by the inner man. This was the very description of Jesus' own life-experience: "Not my will, but thine be done." Later Christians misunderstood this phenomenon by declaring it the incarnation of God's spirit, mind and Will in the historic Jesus. The truth is to be found in a more actual description when it is claimed that when an individual's will is surrendered (abandoned) to the Will of God, there is manifested the reign of God in the inward parts of the individual.

The Kingdom of God, however, is also "without" you, i.e., outside of you, in the interpersonal aspects of living, in the quality of society. When individuals experience release from sin and begin to live not only renewed personal lives but also redeemed and rejuvenated social life, a new culture emerges; new social patterns are created, and the mores of Kingdom-quality individuals take on Kingdom attributes. Then the Kingdom is here. Such resulting group life was known soon after Jesus' day on earth as *koinonia,* or fellowship. There was a spirit and a friendliness in the give and take of that social life that was different, of higher quality, of Kingdom dimensions. The true Christian is the fruit of the spirit at work in group living.

"The kingdom of God is at hand" (cf. Matthew 4:17b, 10:7). One need not physically die, or await some cosmic intervention of God, in order to participate in the Kingdom of God. It is at hand; all one need do is to lay hold on it. The Kingdom of God is present. It begins now. Now is the time for the total commitment of individuals and societies to the reign of God. In such a mood of expectancy and optimism, one need only step out in faith and sin no more, and thereafter live "as though" the Kingdom was already here, and it is . . . to the extent of the sincerity and integrity of the individual and the group.

For Jesus, in his day, the evidences for its present reality were to be found in the exorcism of demons, the recovery of sight to the blind, the restoration of the ability to walk to the lame, the effective cleansing of the leper and the insane, the unclogging of ears to hearing, the resurrection of the dead to earthly living, and as for the poor, the gospel was being preached to everyone without regard for personal strength and vigor (cf. Luke 4). Today, such evidences are not as valuable for proofs as the Godlike lives of ordinary people guided by His spirit.

"In that day the kingdom will come" (cf. Matthew 16:28b). Truly the Kingdom of God is a present reality, yet it is not at home amidst the present order of things. Its maturation will come in some future time.

The whole question of Jesus' own apocalyptic has been thoroughly studied in recent years. The crux of the problem seems to be this: Did Jesus actually believe the vivid apocalypticism of Mark 13? Or is that passage an expression of the faith of the Judaistic early church? Had the Jewish-Christian churches completely misunderstood Jesus? Had they allowed their inherited faith to shine through their records regarding the message of Jesus? For if Jesus believed what is recorded about his teaching on the subject, he was as sadly mistaken as his followers;

for the Messiah did not come on clouds of heaven during their earthly lifetime (Matthew 24:30).

A saying which appears far more in keeping with Jesus' general mood and thought is this: "Watch therefore, for you do not know on what day your Lord is coming" (Matthew 24:42, cf. Mark 13:32). And again, "for the Son of man is coming at an hour you do not expect" (Matthew 24:44*b*). Its coming, therefore, in Jesus' thought rested with God. In His good time God will bring in the new order destined to replace the existing scheme.

Whether the time and method of its coming are cataclysmic or evolutionary is still a debatable question. The followers of Jesus have never solved the problem to its ultimate conclusion. As in the case of individual salvation, so in the case of social change, there appear to be two means, the violent cataclysmic and the peaceful evolutionary. Variations of this twofold means have been and are still held by faithful members of the Church. There is very little doubt, however, that the early church members expected a cosmic event during their earthly lifetimes commensurate to their own sudden experiences. Only when the Messiah failed to return "on clouds of heaven" did the church membership begin to toy with other descriptions and concepts, as well as with other explanations of the future part of the Kingdom of God.

Jesus conceived of this Kingdom, by whatever means it came, to be man's supreme object for striving. It was not man-built, nor was it merited by righteous imitation. It was no human utopia, nor was it a perfect society. Rather, for Jesus it was the complete rule of the holy and eternal God over the souls and fellowship of men. The revolutionary aspect of it was not that it was for the rich, the wise or the good, as man would have it, but that it was reserved for those of contrite heart and penitent spirit. The conditions for entrance were ethical and not national, faith and not obedience, grace and not the works of the Law, a matter of the will and not chiefly of the mind. The Kingdom of God was the reality of salvation, both for the individual and for society.

To summarize the matter one would have to say that Jesus started with the concept of the Kingdom which John the Baptist proclaimed. Then Jesus became more and more content to leave questionable apocalyptic elements to God. In the meanwhile, Jesus began to challenge men to that moral and spiritual change without which they could neither enter nor share in the blessings of the new age of the Kingdom. The framework of Jesus' concept is certainly Jewish, and his ethical emphasis is at least Jewish in origin. Yet his thinking and knowledge concerning the Kingdom show evidences of having passed through his own vigorous religious insights and experiences into a fresh concept of the Kingdom. The Jewish concept was thereby completely transformed into one of universal appeal.

For Jesus the Golden Age was in the near future. Any present aspect of it was partial and somewhat blurred. Yet it was a present privilege to live in the first stages of that Great New Day. In such confidence Jesus himself lived, believing in and expecting the ultimate and complete victory of God and His righteousness.

Himself

One finds Jesus always talking about the Kingdom of God, and rarely about the Messiah, and even more rarely about himself. There has always been a scholarly problem over separating the thought of Jesus from that of the Gospel writers, and from that which the Gospel writers thought Jesus thought.

Certainly Jesus had no grandiose ideas of himself in his childhood. As it has been dramatically conceived, if Jesus had gone about in a typical boyhood fashion, bragging on his messiahship, the first mud puddle would have served as a fine washbasin wherein village bullies would have washed his face. They would not have taken Jesus' childish boasting seriously. The Scriptures support this childhood lack of information on Jesus' part by their reference to Mary's keeping all her memories to herself (Luke 2:19).

At the age of twelve, when next we catch a glimpse of Jesus, we do not see him in his full-blown messiahship. True, we see him a typically curious boy, asking questions, asserting his new freedom, having become a *bar mizvah* (a son of the covenant). In preparation for this signal event in a boy's life, a precocious child like Jesus would not have been satisfied with the process of sheer memorization. He would want to know and come sincerely to believe the faith he was expected to profess with his lips. To what extent he was precocious is still a good question.

Sometime during these awakening and sensitive years Jesus appears to have become aware of his sonship. At least he wanted to be a son of God, and he hoped God would so accept and treat him. This idea may have come to Jesus as a psychological transference at the time of Joseph's death when he was still a boy at heart, weighed down with a man's job and responsibility in a matter of hours. He still needed a father's wisdom and guidance. And when the earthly father had passed beyond the veil, the reality and nearness of the Heavenly Father took on a deep emotional significance.

Of course, he may have been toying with the belief of his own sonship as he pondered the idea that since Israel was the chosen people and God was the Father of that chosen people, then God was his personal Father, as He was for all his chosen people. The new element in this thought was that Jesus took the Fatherhood of God a bit more seriously and applied it to a personal relationship and experience. At first Jesus may have thought of himself as one of many sons of the Heavenly Father; but as he grew older and more sensitive he began to sense a uniqueness in his own experience of the Father and in his own relationship to Him.

Just when in his life Jesus became aware of the Suffering Servant of II Isaiah (chapter 61) is unknown. Certainly this was his choice Scripture when he was called upon to preach his first message in his home synagogue after that momentous experience in and beyond the Jordan. Had he been drawn to this passage all during his alert boyhood? Had this passage, which was rarely read in his hearing, come as a "revelation" to his own sense of mission in life? We cannot be sure. We can only note how significant it became in his public ministry, not only as to his messages but also to his philosophy and manner of living.

It would appear that up to the moment of his baptism Jesus did not have any clear-cut sense of mission or of self-importance. As a member of the chosen people, created in the image of God, Jesus simply took the great teachings of Israel about the Fatherhood of God and the brotherhood of man more personally and seriously. Sincerely he sought to grow up as a child of God, ever increasing into the likeness of God. As God became more fatherly toward him, he sought earnestly to measure up to being a son of God. No wonder it could be said of him: "And Jesus increased in wisdom and in stature, and in favor with God and man" (Luke 2:52).

Then the unexpected happened! In a moment of utter commitment when he abandoned his will to the Father's, the "call" came. The Father's presence was most vivid, and the voice from heaven said: "Thou art my beloved son." The earnest yearning of his young soul came to fulfillment. In faith he had subjected his willful life to his Father, and his sonship was assured. Just how much this feeling is tied up with his parable of the Prodigal Son is a real question. The startling aspect of the experience is to be seen in the psychological connections which lie between this voice from heaven and the Satanic words, "*If* thou art . . ." Thus Jesus "came to himself," "to his mission" and "to his message." What had happened to him could happen to others, and his mission was to share this glorious experience as the "good news" of God unto salvation, not only personally but socially.

As a son Jesus would now live like a son. Sonship required faith and duty, fellowship and responsibility. In almost childlike conscientiousness, Jesus placed his life into the hands of God, to be used at His discretion. Such childlike faith we see in Jesus before and certainly after his experience of baptism. His prayer life is evidence of his constant communication and companionship with God.

Life for Jesus was one long mysterious adventure unfolding under the wise direction of the Father. Such guidance is evident in his great moments of decision: in the wilderness, on the mount of Transfiguration, in the garden of Gethsemane and in the momentous three hours on Golgotha. "Not my will but thine be done" (cf. Luke 22:42). Or again, "Father into thy hands I command my spirit" (cf. Luke 23:46).

Compassion for people also came from this filial relationship. The more one socializes with another the more each becomes like the other. In this case Jesus became increasingly more Godlike. And compassion for people became a characteristic of each. Could it be that it was as Jesus' compassion grew with his insights into the needs of men that he became aware of his possible messiahship? Did Jesus awaken to a new concept of messiahship? Certainly he never considered himself the incarnation of the popular concept of the Messiah, with its political and military core and characteristics.

The Messiah as Jesus conceived him was one who was sent by God to proclaim the "good news." God had been trying to get through to mankind ever since creation. We see Jesus thinking this through more thoroughly at the time of his so-called "temptations." For Jesus, therefore, the Messiah was to proclaim that eternal life and the Kingdom of God are not acquired by the amassing of adequate material goods, such as food, raiment, shelter and much property, but by the acquisition of character, on the part of both the individual human being and the society established by such redeemed individuals. Only through the word proclaimed by God will the secret of righteousness and righteous living among one's fellows be divulged. Only when men will the Will of their Father-God will they taste of life abundant.

The Messiah was to keep himself in the background, for true

righteousness came not through personal loyalties of many followers but through confidence and concentration in God and His Way. He must not distract from God's intent in his messianic mission by grandiose appeals for popular support; he must keep forever humble, no matter how forthright must be his message.

Jesus came to realize that he must help people see that their own salvation as well as that of their society cannot come by compulsion and the methods of force, but only by the subtle means of example and personal testimonies whereby the power of God may be transmitted from person to person throughout the world unto its divine transformation.

It would appear that Jesus gradually became aware of this unique mission and message: we see him therefore declaring that "a greater than the Temple is here" (cf. Matthew 12:6), "a greater than Jonah" is here (cf. Matthew 12:41) and "a greater than Solomon" is standing before men. Such authority Jesus began to feel he could exert because what he proclaimed were God's words, not his own. As God's son, and in a true sense the Messiah, Jesus felt he had a right to be heard and obeyed, even though he rejected the methods of compulsion. In the majesty of such authority, he forthrightly presented himself in a triumphant entry into the Holy City as the first of a series of deliberate and skillfully planned events to present dramatically the Word of God to the world. With equally strong feelings he cleansed the Temple on the next day. Without fear and with great dignity he confronted the high priest and his advisers on the following day, whereon his authority was brought in question. Thus in quiet solemnity he confronted death on a cross in the garden of Gethsemane, and "sweated blood" over it. And in stately mien he proceeded under terrific physical stress to carry manfully his cross to Golgotha.

Jesus died every inch the Messiah he came to know and to believe he was. Yet first and foremost he was a son of God, made in the image of God. Then the Suffering Servant through whom God revealed His love for His Chosen People. And only finally did he accept the Messiahship, when the content and meaning of the mission and message of that Messiah was changed to conform to that which Jesus discerned to be the intention of God for the transformation of the world for all time.

Herein we have stated as clearly as can be discerned the various doctrines whereupon Jesus established his faith and practice.

CHAPTER VIII

THE FAITH THAT MOTIVATED HIM

More subtle than a man's teachings or the objective statements of his apparent doctrinal beliefs are the attitudes and guiding principles which motivate his every action and uttered word. What we are seeking to accomplish in this chapter is to push back our question to its source: to those basic assumptions, guiding principles, which directed Jesus' attitudes and actions, and to discover thereby the essence of his faith.

First there was his basic belief in a God—Jesus assumed the reality of God. Second, there was the fundamental acceptance of earthly living as real, in all its parts: material, fleshly, intellectual and spiritual. At no time did Jesus ever doubt or discredit the earth and all its natural aspects and laws; he simply accepted its reality. Third, there was the assumption that man's life was dependent upon at least a three-way fellowship: man and his God, God and His creatures, and man and his fellow men. For Jesus, there could be no adequate or satisfying life devoid of any one of these three interpersonal relationships. Fourth, there was Jesus' assumption of man's reliance upon the Providence of God, in the abundance of nature to provide food, raiment and shelter.

Every culture has had its code of law, and every religion its commandments, as ethical buoys to help make man aware of his limitations and sins. The Jew, and therefore the people among whom Jesus was born, had the Ten Commandments. In the defining of these laws lies the sinfulness of legalism. Jesus saw this. Thereupon he stated the only commandments which God places upon man: love of God and love of neighbor. These Two Commandments were the only "musts" demanded by Jesus. For him they were the focal points from which all righteous living emanated. These Two Commandments were the generating factors in life that made for God-like living. Jesus believed and trusted them because, for him, they were demanded by God; they cannot be avoided, neglected or ignored. They were demand-commitments made in love.

The position of Jesus in regard to these Two Commandments is in marked contrast to the Judaic fundamental which was a matter of covenant. As understood and believed by the Judaism of Jesus' day, man's relationship to God was one of covenant. Man confessed his guilt and promised to obey in return for God's promise of total reconciliation and personal redemption. Jesus, on the other hand, appears to indicate that the relationship was one not of bargaining and covenanting but of love, respect and understanding between the two parties involved. For Jesus the relationship was founded upon feelings toward one another rather than upon intellectual agreements bonded and sealed as business contracts. This is significant, as we proceed to indicate what appear, on the basis of extant records, to be Jesus' guiding principles and attitudes.

What the present writer is attempting to establish is that set of principles and attitudes which motivated Jesus' every act and utterance. Therefore, before proceeding to state these principles and their correlative attitudes as they are discovered, a word regarding the use of the word "principle" is in order. Philosophically, the word "principle" denotes a moving cause or power whereby "being" manifests itself, and whereby phenomena can be reasonably explained. The usual definition is stated in this wise: a "principle" is that which is inherently motivating in something. It is in this general sense that we wish to use the word as we seek to indicate the principles that motivated Jesus' words and deeds.

One further word of explanation is also due in order to clarify the present approach to the subject. The basic principle will be stated first, and this will be followed by a series of correlative attitudes, each of which will be stated as concisely and cogently as possible. Therefore, the dual aim of this chapter will be accomplished as intertwining concepts. The reader, however, must never lose sight of the fact that the intangible reality which the words and concepts are seeking to describe and explain is the important factor.

Principle 1: In the Beginning God

The first principle to be stated is this: In the beginning God—the God who conceives, creates, maintains and orders all. This was fundamental in Jesus' faith, in both his thought and his action. Jesus moved out into life, personal and social, upon a base of the reality of God. As we stated earlier, Jesus never seemed to have doubted the existence of God. Neither did Jesus become concerned with the theological attributes of the Deity, such as omniscience and infinity. Jesus regarded Him as a Person with whom mankind could have fellowship and understanding.

Moving out from this basic principle we note the following attitudes, which appear to express the faith of Jesus fundamentally.

a) GOD IS A PERSON.—First of all, Jesus regarded God as a Person, one he had met, who could be known, loved and served. For many this may seem axiomatic, but it is important while pagans regard the Deity as a force or power inherent in the cosmos. Yet that which conceives, creates, maintains and orders all has the characteristics of personality. Thus the early Hebrews conceived of God as a Person in whose image man was fashioned.

This Person Jesus regarded as a Father; and as an obedient son Jesus sought to live. Jesus and God were in constant fellowship; they appeared to love each other, respect each other, and mutually sought the welfare of each other. For Jesus this entailed man's filial piety and willingness to do the Will of the Heavenly Father. Such a frank and sincere relationship would, Jesus thought, produce a righteousness in man's attitudes and actions that would mark the individual as a son of God, and the resulting society as the Kingdom of God. In modern parlance, it was a "we" relationship that made Jesus and God one, *not* a oneness of substance—as was the Church's feeble and unfortunate attempt to explain the rare identity of the two persons.

b) GOD AS KING, LEGISLATOR AND JUDGE.—Since Jesus accepted God's rule over all matters, he regarded Him as King, Legislator and Judge. Jesus lived in a monarchial society; it was natural for him to think of God in such symbolism. But there is an eternal verity in this concept, for God is not elected to office, nor can He be dismissed or retired. God is an eternal ruler. He is King.

As King He is also Legislator. It was He who conceived the laws of the universe. Man only discovers and describes them. Since God established all law, it is up to man, according to Jesus, to discover them and to live in agreement with them, not as an unwilling and disciplined slave but as a wise person who sees the rightness, security and truth in such action.

As King and Lawgiver, God is also Judge. In fact, Jesus almost goes so far as to say that God is the only Judge: "Judge not, that you be not judged" (Matthew 7:1, cf. Luke 6:37). The fact of God's Judgeship is the natural corollary of His kingship and His legislative powers. When man lives in the awareness of these attitudes, he lives differently. He seeks "the higher law." He endeavors to obey the will of God. He does not fear the injustices of his fellow men, for they will be judged and prosecuted by the Heavenly Judge; and man's judgments and imprisonments do not break the spirit of the sons of God.

Yet as Ruler, Legislator and Judge, God is fatherly, according to Jesus' experience. He is no benevolent despot; rather, He is a friendly person. This concept and attitude on Jesus' part reflects high praise for Joseph, whatever his relationship to Jesus was. Jesus appears to personalize the father-concept of Judaism. Not only is God the Father of His chosen people as a group, but he is also the personal spiritual Father of each individual—and again, not only of the individual Jew, but God is the Father of every human being, of whatever race or clime.

c) GOD KNOWS ALL, AND KNOWS BEST.—A further attitude which stems from this basic principle is this: since God is the conceiver, creator and maintainer of all life and all matter, then He *knows all,* and *knows best.* It seems almost trite to state that fact, but it is a part of the inherent nature of Jesus' faith. Paul in a later day pointed up this basic attitude by saying: "Do not be conformed to this world but be transformed by the renewal of your mind . . ." (Romans 12:2). Or again, "Have this mind among yourselves, which you have in Christ Jesus" (Philippians 2:5).

Jesus took the position that God knows all and knows best as to how, what, when, where and why. Therefore, it was Jesus' will to "think God's thoughts after Him." Moreover, it would appear that Jesus was so successful in this attunement of minds that his disciples from that day to this have completely identified the two and smothered it in a doctrine of "incarnation." Yet such "incarnation" was not in his awareness, nor was it his intent. Simply stated, Jesus assumed that for his personal maturation and happiness he must attune his thoughts and attitudes to the wisdom and truth of his Heavenly Father, God. This being true for him, all pertinent acts and teachings which stem from this basic attitude were only natural for Jesus, and he gave intellectual and ethical expression to them.

d) MAN CAN DEPEND UPON GOD'S PROVIDENCE.—Since God is the creator, maintainer and orderer of all, man should be able to, and can, depend upon His Providence. Thus Jesus could speak of the birds of the air and the foxes of the wood. He could give positive expression to belief in divine concern for the health and growth of His human sheep. God provides for all His creatures. Thus Jesus lived: "The Son of man has nowhere to lay his head" (Matthew 8:20), or, again, "Make the people sit down" (John 6:10), and bring me the lad's lunch. Or again, "The labourer is worthy of his hire" (Luke 10:7*b*, A.V.). Simply stated, Jesus gave expression in word and deed to the attitude that God provides the essentials of life; therefore man is to trust God. From this basic principle emanated many of Jesus' fundamental attitudes of life.

Principle 2: God Created the Earth

A second principle that appears to lie behind Jesus' words and deeds is this: *God created the earth.* Jesus accepted and believed this. In later centuries the Marcionites refused to believe that the Heavenly Father of the Lord Jesus Christ created the earth, which they regarded as fundamentally evil and full of misery and pain. Jesus, however, did not find the earth evil. Nor did he regard it only as the source and habitation of all disease, suffering and loathsomeness. To Jesus, God created the earth. As offspring of this basic principle, the following attitudes seem to come normally and naturally.

a) THE EARTH IS GOOD, BEAUTIFUL AND FRIENDLY.—First of all, since God created the earth, the earth is good, beautiful and friendly. There is abundant evidence (cf. Matthew 6:26 f., 8:20, 13:3 f., etc.) to show that all of Jesus' life appears to have been flooded with the joy of earth. He felt a part of his Father's world. Every flower and creature caught his attention; he loved the great out of doors. Everything was his to enjoy. The flowers, the birds, the foxes, the sunsets all caught his eye and stimulated his appreciation. Everything commonplace awakened his adoration. The earth was beautiful, more beautiful than "Solomon in all his glory" (Matthew 6:29).

The earth was good . . . That was saying a lot in a land where people went to bed hungry every night. If Jesus had lived in abundant Greece or the fertile Nile Valley, one could see why he would think that the earth was good; but not so in Palestine. Yet it *was* good, simply because God created it; and if it became at times harsh and foreboding, that was man's fault, not God's.

Tramping the hillsides of Galilee and standing upon the mountaintops gave Jesus views of the Mediterranean to the west and the blue Sea of Tiberius to the east. Jesus felt very friendly toward the earth round about him. Though he failed to travel outside of Palestine, he envisioned the earth everywhere to be wonderful as he knew it. Others knew that there were areas in the

Empire where nature was at its best, and far superior to that which Jesus knew. Yet Jesus sensed that the whole earth was friendly, good and truly beautiful.

b) MAN SHOULD RESPECT THE EARTH.—There is immediately another attitude expressed: that man should appreciate, maintain and respect the earth whereon he lives. Since it is God's good earth, Jesus felt a deep sense of appreciation for it. Beyond his response to it as beautiful, and good, he recognized his responsibility to maintain it. He ever sought to help his agricultural countrymen to take good care of the earth they tilled; this was especially necessary when he recognized the evidences of human disregard for and ravaging of the soil through ignorance, carelessness and selfishness. It was for him to help his agricultural friends to restore and maintain that priceless commodity, top soil. Their dietary laws concerning spotless animals prodded them into careful husbandry; yet through indigence and ignorance they did not care with the same concern for the health of the soil. Jesus' attitude toward the earth and its products was very favorable; therefore, he sought to establish within the souls of men those divine motives which would express themselves in healthy and enlightened attitudes and acts toward God's gift to men, the good earth. He sought to build up a sense of respect for the earth and all its component parts—plants, birds, beasts and fish.

c) ALL PROPERTY IS A STEWARDSHIP.—This leads to another fundamental attitude which stems from this same basic principle: that all property is a stewardship rather than a personal possession. Since God created and continues to maintain all life, all is His. Nothing is ours to possess utterly. We are privileged to till a portion of the earth, to use in divers manners the products and inhabitants of earth, but everything we seem to possess is but a stewardship for which we shall have to give an account. (Note the various parables wherein Jesus indicated this; cf. Luke 12: 15–21, 16:1–9, 19:12–28, Matthew 25:14–30.) This belief in the stewardships of life and matter is evident in his belief in providence, in his ascetic way of life and in his pleading for the storing of heavenly riches rather than building bigger barns (cf. Luke 12:21). This was and still is the wholesome attitude of the nomad; and Jesus believed that such a sense of stewardship was good for man in his relationship to earth and its creatures including man. "If you would be mature, go, sell what you possess and give it to the poor . . ." (cf. Matthew 19:21).

Principle 3: Man Made in God's Image

Reminding ourselves about what constitutes a principle, we move on to a third motivation in Jesus' faith: man was created by God *in His own image*. This statement we traditionally accept as a fact of divine revelation which the Hebrews stated in their Scriptures. But Jesus did not accept merely the revelation; he assumed it. It was a part of his inherent relationship to his fellow men, and it found expression in the following attitudes.

a) MAN IS CROWN AND SUMMIT OF GOD'S CREATIVITY.—For Jesus, God's creative activity came to glorious heights in the creation of man, and Jesus approached each individual with that fact in mind. No matter how degraded or despondent the person was, Jesus saw him as a child of God. Jesus never beheld the individual in his present state of being. He looked always into the future, to what this person could and would become. His present compassion blended into expectant joy.

b) EACH INDIVIDUAL IS A SON OF GOD.—Thus, a corollary attitude on Jesus' part was that he recognized each human being as a son of God. He treated each individual as worthy of such respect. Created in the divine image, each person was truly a child of God pregnant with potentialities of divine likeness. The sonship of others was like his own. To each man God was Heavenly Father, to whom filial piety was due. Man need only recognize his sonship, and lovingly serve.

c) RESPECT FOR PERSONALITY.—A third and final attitude, closely related to the two above, stems from this basic principle:

as God's son, each one will and must have respect for personality as such.

(A) First of all, this involves respect for the total person: body, mind and soul. As has been indicated earlier, for Jesus and the Jews a person is a unity. The trilogy of body, mind and spirit is Hellenistic in concept, not Judaic.

(i) Thus, respect for personality involved respect for the miraculous organism called the body. Proper health measures for the welfare of others are involved in this basic attitude. Therefore Jesus was concerned not only for his own bodily health but for the healthy faculties of the bodies of those who came to him for healing. Everywhere he went he expressed this attitude in his healing ministry, in his interest in the sick, the maimed and the blind.

(ii) Yet the physical body was not the whole person. Jesus never forgot respect for the intellectual capabilities of others; in fact, he appears to have deliberately sought to tease and challenge the minds of men to greater heights and depths of insight. Thus he spars with a lawyer concerning the Commandments (Mark 12:28–34, Matthew 22:34–40, Luke 10:25–28, 20:39–40). He uses the parable as a mode of teaching to express great concepts and truths which a concise abstract statement would never adequately reveal (cf. Matthew 13:10–17, Luke 8:9–10). It took intellectual effort to gather his implications from this method. Jesus never talked down to his fellow men, despite their lack of formal education, and his occasional exasperation with them, as evidenced by his famous exclamation, "O men of little faith" (Matthew 6:30, 8:26; cf. Luke 8:25, 12:28).

(iii) Even more important than these two aspects of the person was "the inner man," what the Greeks called "the soul." Jesus had great respect for this part of man. Here was where lay the "sickness" in man's existence. Jesus talked of "abundant life," of "entering the kingdom," and the author of the fourth Gospel has him speak of "eternal life." Such life was not the lot of the average individual; in fact, no one seems to have shared in the fullness of life as Jesus had come to experience it. This was the good news he had to share with others: they could taste of the *joie de vivre* as he had come to experience it. It was because he had thrilled to its pulsating joy that he wanted it for others. He had put his finger on the key to the soul's liberation: man's relationship to his God and to his fellow man in terms of love. Thus his proclamation of the two great commandments (Mark 12:28–34, Matthew 22:34–40, Luke 10:25–28, 20:39–40) and his respect and concern for the souls of men.

He respected the whole man, but spiritual food was of more consequence than physical sustenance and intellectual questing. "For what does it profit a man if he gains the whole world and loses or forfeits himself?" (Luke 9:25, 12:15, Matthew 16:26.) "And do not fear those who kill the body but cannot kill the soul; rather fear him who can destroy both soul and body in hell" (Matthew 10:28). Thus runs Jesus' thought on respect for personality. "You are of more value than many sparrows" (Matthew 10:31, cf. Luke 12:7). And, if it is a choice between other creatures and man, save man, sacrifice all else. For man is made in God's image; he is God's son and a fellow heir with Christ (cf. Romans 8:17). Man, the zenith of God's creative genius, is too precious to be expendable. He is a miracle to be revered, to be respected.

(B) Respect for personality opens up Jesus' attitudes toward the outcast and the less fortunate individuals in society.

(i) In Jesus' day this attitude of respect took notice of womanhood and childhood as few of the world did. Certainly in the Near and Middle East womanhood and childhood were expendable: only the male child was important. Jesus sought to change all this simply by giving expression to this basic attitude which stemmed from one of his principles of faith-living. A woman was a person as much as any male. It was only by divine plan that she inhabited a different body with different characteristics. Souls, personalities, characters were nonsexed. Therefore, respect for the male involved respect for the female. Respect for adults also meant respect for children and youths. With these attitudes,

Jesus expressed a religious faith that brought democracy in its wake.

(ii) Such respect for personality, however, involved concern and respect for the sick in body and mind (cf. Luke 14:12-14). It meant compassion for the drug addict, the insane and the outcast, which society had spurned and driven in many instances into the cemeteries and waste places of parched Palestine. It also drew attention to the criminal, the enemy and the immoral person. Respect for personality meant concern for every individual. It gave meaning and action to the scriptural question: "Am I my brother's keeper?" (Genesis 4:9c.) No human being could henceforth be ignored, subjected, maltreated or arbitrarily disposed of. The ramifications of this fundamental attitude of Jesus' faith are still unfolding in our day.

(iii) Respect for personality also indicated concern with such matters as the interpersonal relationships to be found in marriage, labor relations and neighborhood living. "As you wish that men would do to you, do so to them" (Luke 6:31) found expression in Jesus' words and deeds—as it has in the literature of practically every religion on the planet.

(iv) Finally, such respect for personality became concerned with the spirit and atmosphere involved in interracial, interfaith, intercultural and international relations. No better comment by Jesus to reveal this over-all attitude could be had than this: "Unless your righteousness exceeds that of the scribes and Pharisees, you will never enter the kingdom of heaven" (Matthew 5:20). It is this almost unprecedented attitude which has characterized Jesus' faith, and that of the Christian Church.

Principle 4: Man in Need of Maturation

A fourth basic principle is that man, born with a free will, stands in need of maturation and redemption. In Jesus' mind, as in ours, every human being falls far short of God's intention for man's welfare and happiness. This was the price God had to pay in His endeavor not to have puppets and automatons but human beings. To be created in His image, man must be granted that free will and ability to mature or to degrade himself which alone makes it possible for man to be a *person* like God, not a *machine* whose every act is manipulated by circumstances beyond its control. He spoke of man as sinner (cf. Luke 15:7, 13:1–5), yet at no time did he come out with the traditional Christian dogma that man was *born in sin*. This was Paul's rather unfortunate conception of the plight of man (cf. Romans 3:9). Perhaps we can understand the implications of Jesus' basic principle here if we consider the corollary attitudes involved.

a) MAN'S BASIC INCOMPLETENESS.—Jesus assumed man's basic incompleteness as a person; man was pictured as selfish, ignorant, immature and willful. To say this was not to say that man is by nature a sinner. The individual has not yet tasted God's intended life for him. To say this was not to blame his sin upon Adam's sin, nor to claim that Adam's defection was inherited as physical difficulties can be inherited. Jesus recognized the incompleteness of each person in turn. Some of that incompleteness was due to lack of knowledge or experience; some to man's selfishness and willfulness, which were acts of free will rather than his nature acting irresponsibly.

God in His endeavor to make us in His image had to create us capable of maturation but not already mature. He had to create us with freedom of choice: the ability to choose between good and evil, and to taste the consequences of our choice. He had to make us maneuverable so that we could grow or decay. Therefore, Jesus was more wholesome in his attitude toward man in his state on earth; he truly regarded man as sinner, but only in the sense that man had not yet learned or had willfully failed to measure up to or attain the intent of God, that man had not yet attuned himself to those moral and spiritual laws that bring with them righteousness and happiness.

Thus we see that Jesus accepted man as he was: each individual in his own plight or station of progress toward maturation and Godlikeness. He recognized man's immaturity, lack of

The Faith That Motivated Him 185

fulfillment and occasional separation from God, but Jesus appears never to have bemoaned the fact or to condemn unduly the individual for his plight. Rather, his attitude was more positive, seeking restoration, looking toward growth and maturation for the individual.

b) RELEASE OF MAN'S POTENTIALITIES.—A second corollary attitude is Jesus' approach to the person's need. What one needs is not a new set of manners. This Jesus likened to whited sepulchres (cf. Matthew 23:27-28, Luke 11:44), very polished actions façading the dry bones of a dull character within the human frame. Neither did man need a new example, even his own (Mark 10:17-18, Luke 18:18-19), toward which to strive by disciplined living. Rather, what was needed was the freeing of divine forces latent in the human personality which would unfold into true images of the Godhead. Jesus saw his task not that of a rescuer alone, but more of a liberator. He sought to release the latent powers toward maturity which are part of the very nature of man. Herein we see Jesus' more wholesome attitude toward his fellow men and their circumstances; he saw great possibilities in each person's growth and maturation, whatever the present circumstances.

c) HUMAN BETTERMENT.—A third attitude may be called "human betterment." Jesus saw, anticipated, expected and yearned for the fulfillment of each individual life. What he had experienced he wanted others to experience. This was his glad tidings to hungering humanity. "Blessed are those who hunger and thirst for righteousness, for they shall be satisfied" (Matthew 5:6).

What Jesus saw in such righteousness was the positive maturity of the whole person into the fullness of man's image-nature. The ramifications of this attitude in modern terms would involve acknowledgment of the possibility of man to "increase in wisdom and stature and in favor with God and man" (cf. Luke 2:52). This would be saying in so many words that Jesus saw that individuals could be altruistic, educated, emotionally matured and spiritually redeemed. In such anticipation Jesus approached his fellow men. For this he was often criticized, especially when he associated with those whom some members of society regarded as less-desirables: harlots, publicans, sinners and the mentally deranged. No one was eternally lost, or irretrievable; all had potentialities of greatness, for they were sons and daughters of God.

Principle 5: Faith Is the Key

A fifth basic principle upon which Jesus' faith stood was this: man's fulfillment in God's righteousness is effected through *faith* in God and His Will. This is related to an earlier principle that Jesus assumed that God knew best and therefore His Will was right, good and true. At this juncture we are seeking to state the principle on which, theologians would say, salvation rests—that principle which the Apostle Paul stated in terms of faith and works (cf. Galatians 2:15–20). Paul's finding that man's fulfillment in righteousness was achieved by the undeserved mercy of God through faith was a disciple's discovery of this basic principle of Jesus.

a) CONDUCT IS THE BY-PRODUCT OF CHARACTER.—When we turn from this basic principle to the corollary attitudes, we meet with some of Jesus' most fundamental assumptions. We note first that, for Jesus, conduct is a result or by-product of character, and not vice versa. This seemingly irrational fact is still a puzzle to modern Pharisees, as it was to those in Jesus' day.

It appears to be common for men to believe that one can make one's self over by self-disciplined conduct, by "putting one's best foot forward," as the colloquial expression states. Thus many an individual, as well as society, has led himself into this debacle. The fact is man cannot legislate righteousness either for himself or for his fellow men. Man is either good at the core because of the integration of his soul, or he is not. As Jesus put it: "Either make the tree good, and its fruit good; or make the tree bad, and its fruit bad; for the tree is known by its fruit" (Matthew 12:33).

Jesus recognized all this. He sought to impart this attitude to his hearers. He operated his healing ministry on this premise by going to the heart of the matter in each individual case. Set the person in right relationship to his God and God's Will, and the individual's mental and physical difficulties would ultimately correct themselves. Point up in each case the seat of the trouble and then correct it (cf. Luke 5:23, Matthew 9:5-6). Thus Jesus sought to express this basic principle by means of his attitude toward the ills of mankind.

b) Seek ye first the Kingdom.—A further attitude in direct connection with this principle of redemption was that which saw man's part in the cure. God was the initiator; he stood ever ready to lead men into rightness and fulfillment, but man must first see his need and want maturity, i.e., the Kingdom of God, as Jesus described it. "Seek first his kingdom and his righteousness, and all these things shall be yours as well" (Matthew 6:33).

Therefore, Jesus saw man's need for repentance. But repentance for Jesus was no mere remorsefulness. Repentance involved the act of rethinking. Jesus saw that he must help men see as he had come to see God's way of fulfillment. They had to see, as it were, through God's eyes the way unto maturity in accordance with the inherent laws of health for the body, for the mind, but more for the soul. This adherence came through a form of attunement by means of faith in God and His righteousness. Like the tuning of a musical instrument with a basic tuning fork, each individual must personally and incessantly seek to attune his whole being to the Being of God and His Will for men.

This attunement process gradually attains an "at-one-ment" with God's inherent design for men. It helps the individual to attain his stature as an image of God, and thus makes him a worthy son of God. This was true manhood for Jesus. This was true atonement, also, for which innumerable useless sacrifices had been offered. It can be seen readily that Jesus stood in the line of the prophets, emphasizing the ethical as over against the priestly stress on the ceremonial. He did this because through his own personal experience of God he had been taught that this was true. What God demanded was not new manners but the radiation of those characteristics of a new personality. Such newness was maturity, and came through the practices of faith and attunement.

When one speaks of such attunement, one is not speaking of what might be called "absorption mysticism." Granted that it approximates it when true "at-one-ment" comes; but individual personalities remain forever separate. God is still God, and the image is still the image, and Jesus is still Jesus, and the individual is still himself. God, therefore, is not *in* Jesus, nor is the individual saint absorbed into the Deity, as a raindrop into a lake. Such attunement as we speak of remains true to the tuning-fork symbol. The tone is identical but one is forever the fork, the other the individual instrument.

Only through faith can man attune his will, mind and heart to those of God. Moreover, Jesus conceived of faith as utter self-abandonment to God and His Will. Those who gave up everything in faith would attain fulfillment (cf. Luke 24:25–33). They would be his family (cf. Luke 8:21). They would be able to remove mountains (cf. Matthew 17:20, 21:21). But such faith was rare (cf. Matthew 8:10). Yet it was the key to man's fulfillment in godlikeness.

Principle 6: The Ultimate for Man Is a Natural Goodness

A sixth principle which motivated Jesus' actions and words was this: God's intention for man, created in His image, was that man's personal life be abundant and eternal, a true reflection of God's nature.

We have seen that man's attunement to God's Will, mind and spirit actuates his atonement. Atonement manifests itself in an improved or changed character in man. That improved character then radiates a different and new quality of personality.

The question, then, is "What was God's intention as to character of this new personality in man?" In this Jesus was certain:

The Faith That Motivated Him

God intended man to mature through spiritual communion and attunement into the full and abundant nature of a true son. Jesus assumed that man had been created (or procreated) for ultimate maturation in likeness to God, as a true son of God. This affected Jesus' approach to each individual; he assumed that, at whatever station in life man was at the moment of the encounter, man was capable of growth and improvement toward that personal life that can only be described as abundant and eternal.

Jesus had tasted this abundant life for himself. The ever-increasing awareness of it thrilled him. He believed that it became his experience at the very moment when he abandoned himself completely to the Father in baptism at the hands of John. This *joie de vivre* he came to desire for others; he was convinced that this was the Will of God for every man.

This attunement experience appeared as natural goodness, not as a personal achievement on the part of the individual. It was a by-product of the person's complete surrender to the spirit, mind and Will of God. A former generation spoke of an individual being used "as a channel of God's grace and spirit." This was also an attempt to describe the glorious experience, but it now appears disrespectful and almost insulting to the personality of man, and not in keeping with the nature of God. Rather, what we have is that wonderful fulfillment of man's basic nature as God intended it. Thus the integrity of God, and Jesus, and the individual human being are kept in mutual respect. Each expresses his truest and most righteous nature. The human being acknowledges in humility his own awareness of inadequacy and sinfulness, which has been fortunately recorded in the reports regarding Jesus himself (cf. "Why do you call me good?" Luke 18:18–19, Mark 10:17–18; and ". . . not my will but what thou wilt," cf. Mark 14:36, Matthew 26:39, Luke 22:42). Need we point to our own experiences in two of the Master's parables? (Cf. the Prodigal Son, Luke 15:11–32 and the publican in the Temple, Luke 18:9–14.)

A further attitude is in evidence in the records. Virtue for virtue's sake does not seem to have been clearly stated by Jesus. He continued the age-long custom of indicating the rewards and punishments which were guides to rather inadequately disciplined individuals. Jesus' attitude was concerned with matters of rewards and punishments more than some recent Christians would wish. The ultimate of Jesus' attitude, however, will be to be good for the joy of goodness. To play upon words we can say: we should be good for goodness' sake.

The premise that Jesus built on was that God had a destiny for mankind; the destiny for the individual was to be the image of the Deity. Such an image could come only if man were free to choose for himself that destiny. Only by trial and error, by tasting and observing the consequences of right and wrong choices, through conscious attunement by means of faith and sympathy, was man to arrive ultimately to that true state of maturity for which God created him. Only by such means would man maintain his own integrity and be a person instead of a marionette in the hands of God. God appears divinely wise in His means to this end for the individual human being. Only then would man truly reflect the Father and be a true son.

Principle 7: A Relationship of Love

A seventh principle underlying the faith of Jesus was that God's relationship to man is one of love and respect. Jesus found God to be like that. A Christian who holds the traditional position of the supernatural nature of Jesus would agree immediately. What other relationship could exist between God and the sinless One, between God and His son, between God the Father and God the son? Yet we maintain this was and is the experience of many: "We love, because he first loved us" (I John 4:19). Jesus could agree with the writer of this First Epistle of John when he wrote:

> Beloved, let us love one another; for love is of God, and he who loves is born of God and knows God. He who does not

love does not know God; for God is love. . . . Beloved, if God so loved us, we also ought to love one another. No man has ever seen God; if we love one another, God abides in us and his love is perfected in us. (I John 4:7-8,11-12)

We must recognize an important fact here; the writer of I John was a discoverer with Jesus of this basic principle in life: God loves and respects the individual. Because this is the way of God, so it is the proper way of man with his fellow man.

a) LOVE IS THE LAW OF LIFE.—When we turn to those corollary attitudes which stem from this principle we begin with "Love is the law of life." So Jesus discovered, so he proclaimed; and all who believe will also discover as evidenced by this very quotation from I John. Thus Jesus saw that all the Commandments of Moses could be gathered up into the Two Commandments (Mark 12:28-34 and parallels). All other commandments became unnecessary, for their unconscious fulfillment comes as a by-product of such gracious living.

b) GRACE, UNDESERVED MERCY.—A second attitude which Jesus expressed in this connection was that grace (i.e., undeserved mercy) was an expression of God's love toward man. Jesus noted how God without thought of man's worthiness showered His blessings upon all mankind (cf. Matthew 5:45). In every way God manifested His love upon His creatures for the health and welfare of all. Man was humbled in the presence of such divine benevolence.

c) THE FORGIVING GOD.—A twin attitude to that one just above was the one which assumes the forgiveness of God as an equal expression of His love for mankind. God's forgiveness, Jesus believed, was ever available to the individual. It was upon the basis of this attitude that Jesus felt that his mission in life was "to seek and to save those that were lost, to bring healing not to the well but to the sick" (cf. Luke 5:31-32). This fundamental attitude of Jesus is dramatically portrayed by the apocalyptic writer when he portrays Jesus standing at the door and knocking (Revelation 3:20). Jesus pictured God as a good shepherd who leaves the ninety and nine to seek out the one that has gone astray (cf. Luke 15:3–7, Matthew 18:10–14).

d) AS GOD TREATS MEN, SO MAN WILL TREAT HIS FELLOW MAN.—A further corollary attitude is this: that as God treats men, so man approximating maturation will increasingly treat his fellow man. This was Jesus' statement in the so-called Golden Rule (cf. Luke 6:31, Matthew 7:12). Therefore Jesus informed Peter that a true son of God would forgive "seventy times seven" (cf. Matthew 18:21–22, Luke 17:4). This seems the natural by-product and consequence of attunement through faith. Let us remind ourselves that this was so much the actuality of Jesus' personal experience of God and daily living that his followers down through the ages have mistaken the similarity for the identity, the likeness for the actual.

In the so-called Lord's Prayer we read these words: "And forgive us our debts as we also have forgiven our debtors" (Matthew 6:12). Once again the basic principle of love is expressed. Only as the son forgives can he expect forgiveness from the Father. We know that God will forgive or at least extend forgiveness even if we fail to manifest it in our lives. Yet we have no reason or right to believe that we will receive such forgiveness beyond the measure that we are willing to expend on others. Only by such love and respect as God shows toward men can man measure his own manifestation of God-like love and respect toward others, and therein to approximate his own fulfillment.

e) SUPERIOR RIGHTEOUSNESS.—There was yet one more attitude involved herewith. Jesus said:

> If you love those who love you, what credit is that to you? For even sinners love those who love them. And if you do good to those who do good to you, what credit is that to you? For even sinners do the same. And if you lend to those from whom you hope to receive, what credit is that to you? Even sinners lend to sinners, to receive as much again. But love your enemies, and do good, and lend, expecting nothing in return; and your reward will be great, and *you will*

be sons of the Most High; for he is kind to the ungrateful and the selfish. Be merciful, even as your Father is merciful. (Luke 6:32–36, italics added; cf. Matthews 5:44–48)

Here we see Jesus' attitude more clearly manifested. Immature love is inadequate for high and noble mature living. Attunement approximating the likeness of God's nature will normally and naturally express the love recognized as divine. Thus Jesus said, "Unless your righteousness exceeds that of the scribes and Pharisees, you will never enter the kingdom of heaven" (Matthew 5:20). Connected herewith are the admonitions of Jesus to go the second mile (cf. Matthew 5:41), to turn the other cheek (cf. Luke 6:29, Matthew 5:39), to dispense with the extra cloak (cf. Luke 6:29, Matthew 5:40), and other sayings (cf. Matthew 5:42). These were just plainly expected manifestations of the mature soul, the redeemed person. Many have regarded these injunctions as impractical idealism, but for Jesus and those like him who have tasted gloriously of the new life pulsating within them, this was no idle or ideal talk. This was the evidence of attunement. It should be pointed out that this new life was no result of adoption (as with Paul in Galatians 4:5) or of grafting (cf. Acts 2:33) or even of invasion (cf. Galatians 2:20). Rather, it was the released potentialities latent within each individual's being. God's way, Jesus assumed, was the way of love, which awakens confidence in one's self, faith and trust in others, and hope for the ultimate victory of righteousness and peace within the individual and within society.

Principle 8: A New Society

The next principle which underlies Jesus' faith is this: a mature, or redeemed, individual, as a social creature living in groups, will bring forth a more mature and redeemed society which, because of the reign of God in human hearts and history, is truly the *Kingdom* of God. We see that Jesus' principles and attitudes do not conclude with the individual; they involve social views. Herein the fourth Gospel appears to fail, for the author dared to change Jesus' concept of the *Kingdom* to that of *eternal life,* i.e., from the individual-societal to the exclusively individual. This Jesus did not do, nor did he intend to manifest such an attitude. Jesus' attitude incorporated the resulting social change he anticipated, which he likewise expected to be a part of the abundant life of man.

As the individual lives, tastes, develops and shares the joys and sorrows of life, a community with a very definite character all its own comes into being. Such a statement is axiomatic for all sociologists. Yet it needs to be stated boldly, for it is this fact that becomes one of Jesus' basic principles of word and action. Change the individual, change society. Mature the individual, mature the ways people treat and regard each other in the community relationships of life. Redeem the individual, redeem society and slough off those social ills and adolescent activities and attitudes which hamper happy and wholesome group living. This was the chain-reaction by-product of growth and maturation in the divine destiny of mankind.

a) THE KINGDOM OF GOD.—Jesus projected and prophesied a Kingdom of God on earth as in heaven. Judaism had inherited this truth from Hebraic origins. The Hebraic concept was described as "the seed of Abraham," "the chosen people" of the covenant; and now, Jesus and John the Baptist spoke of the Kingdom of God. In behalf of this social manifestation of a mature community Jesus prayed, preached, healed and died. This expectation became his all-consuming passion, once he had tasted and envisioned it. A new day was dawning. In this, Jesus was apocalyptic to some extent. Yet he perceived this new humanity and community not as something imposed, miraculously let down from a supernatural heaven, as a later writer saw it (cf. Revelation 21:1 f.), but as a way of life evolving as an inevitable by-product of the divine Will and purpose working itself out through awakened latent souls of individuals in social fellowship and co-operation.

The Faith That Motivated Him

b) THE KINGDOM IS GOD'S.—As we have noted Jesus' attitude regarding the means of manifesting the reign of God in society, we turn now to a second fundamental attitude. Not only did Jesus inherit the term "the Kingdom of God" but he assumed the correctness of the concept. The new society was *God's*. Evidence has been presented earlier to show that Jesus spoke constantly of "the kingdom *of God*" (italics added). Scholars feel that it was due to Matthew's conservatively disciplined mind that compelled him to speak of it as "the kingdom *of heaven*" (italics added). One can note the authoritative words of the historic Jesus in the fourth Gospel by the rare use of the term "the kingdom of God" in contrast to the frequent use of the Johannine equivalent, "eternal life." It is only later Christian theologians who stress the Kingdom as Christ's (or Jesus'). Jesus always regarded it as God's Kingdom. After all, it was first conceived by God, and presumably predestined by the Heavenly Father. God was its Ruler, God's Will its law, God's spirit its atmosphere and mood.

c) IT IS A KINGDOM.—"The kingdom of God" is *a kingdom*. Already in this chapter we have noted this fact. It is no parliamentarian government. God cannot be outvoted; He holds the eternal veto in His power. It is a kingdom; and as the concept implies, it is totalitarian in form. Man humbly waits upon the benevolent character of God for wholesome living individually and socially toward the maturation and fulfillment of divine destiny. This was what Jesus thought. Upon such an attitude Jesus spoke and took action. The fourth-Gospel writer, who failed to see the societal implications of the concept, nevertheless caught this attitude of Jesus when he quotes Jesus as saying: "I can do nothing on my own authority; as I hear, I judge; and my judgment is just, because I seek not my own will but the will of him who sent me. If I bear witness to myself, my testimony is not true; there is another who bears witness to me, and I know that the testimony which he bears to me is true." (John 5:30–32.)

d) THE CITIZENS OF THE KINGDOM ARE NOT SLAVES.—As in the

case of the individual, so in the case of society God did not allow Himself to become mechanical or otherwise a manipulator of human affairs. He was no doting parent seeking to impose His wiser counsel upon the immature or inexperienced, or even upon those who were willfully antagonistic to Him. Only by the interaction of growing persons could individuals as well as the group mature into the wholesome destiny God had predestined for all mankind. Here we must note that the mistakes are not inherent evils in the nature of man or society but the inevitable fruits of immaturity, ignorance, selfishness and downright sin. Only through the process of experience, covering a seemingly interminable number of millennia, will God and man see the ultimate consummation of the New Heaven and the New Earth (cf. Revelation 21:1). Of course, the apocalyptists conceive all this only in terms of a sudden imposition upon present society because their personal experience of individual fulfillment happened to come to them suddenly and seemingly imposed from above, even though regarded as a free gift of God. The question of how apocalyptic Jesus was is still a moot one. It is this writer's belief as the result of sympathetic research that Jesus was more of a "gradualist" than his disciples and the membership of the later Church would give him credit for being. Thus we catch a glimpse of the social destiny of man as Jesus believed God planned it in terms of the Kingdom of God.

Principle 9: Death Is a Fact

"Death is a fact" was another basic principle upon which Jesus' faith was founded. Jesus assumed the fact. He worked in regard to it. Yet interestingly, he never considered it the end of human life. Jesus thought of the fact of death in connection not only with the body, but with the mind and soul as well. Even though he may have maintained the Jewish concept of the unity of man, yet he recognized in the physically living the intellectually (cf. Matthew 23:27) and the spiritually (cf. Matthew

8:20) dead. But at no time has it been recorded just what Jesus thought about death, its cause or nature.

a) PHYSICAL DEATH IS A FACT.—Physically, death is a fact: this Jesus accepted. The records indicate that at times loved ones thought he brought back the dead to life. There was the Nain widow's son (Luke 7:11–17), Jairus' daughter (Mark 5:21–24,35–43 and parallels) and Mary and Martha's brother Lazarus (John 11:1–44). Yet in each case we assume that, regardless of what Jesus did, physical death came to each again. At least they do not exist today. There was also the centurion's slave who, "at the point of death" (Luke 7:1–10, cf. Matthew 8:5–10,13 and John 4:46–53), was restored to health before a future fatal moment.

At no place does the record give Jesus' explanation for physical death. He seemed simply to accept it. Paul, on the other hand, had quite another attitude and a very definite explanation for the fact of physical death (cf. Romans 6:12–13). Even though Jesus' fellow Jews called death "sleep," the records show Jesus could distinguish between the two (Mark 5:39).

Furthermore, physical death did not seem to concern Jesus. It was a common occurrence. We must assume that the funeral procession was a quite prevalent sight in that unfortunate country of poverty and squalor. Yet Jesus said: "Do not fear those who kill the body but cannot kill the soul; rather fear him who can destroy both soul and body in hell" (Matthew 10:28). It was with the souls of men that Jesus was most concerned; they must not be allowed to die.

b) JESUS WAS CONCERNED WITH "INWARD" DEATH.—On one occasion a disciple asked to be excused long enough to attend a funeral, but Jesus mildly rebuked him with these words: "Leave the dead bury their own dead" (Matthew 8:20, Luke 9:60). This introduces another attitude of Jesus concerning death. Precisely to what kind of death was he referring in this statement? Was it some kind of intellectual or spiritual death? Is Jesus saying: Let the dull of wit be concerned with the small inconsequentials of life? Or is he saying: Let the insensitive and spiritually dead be concerned with the everyday tasks of the material-centered life? We shall never know just what Jesus meant here, but one thing is sure: he was not asking cadavers to bury the corpse (Matthew 8:20).

It was with these "inward" deaths of man's person that Jesus was most concerned; these must be made alive. For when the person was inwardly alive and alert, the fact of physical death became of no account. Persons in this category who died physically died in the hope and assurance of some form of life after death. To the task of making alive the inward man Jesus set his heart. This was his ministry. This was part of the total reality of "the Kingdom of God" as Jesus saw it.

Death was a fact to Jesus. He took it as a part of the divine plan of life on this planet. Despite the record in the fourth Gospel (John 11:35) as to how Jesus wept at Lazarus' tomb, he remained calm in its presence and sought to help others to do so. And when his own death came he faced up to his own attitudes and faith, and despite the seemingly inherent tug of self-preservation, he placed his inner immortal soul in the hands of God, his Heavenly Father.

Principle 10: Being Is Immortal

Finally, we must recognize one more basic principle upon which Jesus acted and thought. There are seemingly two ways to give literary expression to this principle: (*a*) there is life after death, or more truly, (*b*) being is immortal. What we are attempting to express is the inherent principle in Jesus' faith which says that the personality of the individual is indestructible, immortal; that the death of the body in no way really affects the characteristics, the quality and the reality of the individual human being.

We should remind ourselves at this point of the Judaic concept that, because of the unity of man, death consists of a sort of "suspended animation" of the whole person until some un-

The Faith That Motivated Him

specified day in the future when the dead arise to share in the glorious fulfillment of the reign of God on earth as in heaven. Sadducees were noted (cf. Mark 12:18, Matthew 22:23 and Luke 20:27), we recall, for refusing this much hope for man. For them when a person died physically, that was the end. Death of the body precluded any life of the mind and soul, for man was a unity. The Pharisees, on the other hand, supported the thesis of suspended animation and regarded the dead as only asleep. As one rabbi has said, "This is a biological problem, but not a problem of faith."

We should also state the Hellenistic concept of the matter as it undoubtedly penetrated Galilee where the growing boy of Nazareth became exposed to it. The philosophical inquisitiveness of the Greek mind had made a distinction between the material and the spiritual aspects of man's nature; as a consequence, the Greek could conceive the death of the flesh and the immortality of the soul. And in the centuries which follow the Apostolic Period in the history of the Christian Church this concept was allowed to be developed to extremes. The soul became more real and therefore more important than the flesh. Then the idealism of asceticism broke in upon the Christian thought pattern and distorted the unity of man as God had created him.

a) THE SOUL IS IMMORTAL.—Now, it would appear that Jesus reflected the presumably Galilean blending of the two concepts. As Jesus could conceive of the death of the intellectual and spiritual aspects of man while man was physically very much alive, so Jesus could conceive of the immortality of the "inward man" after the death of the body. Yet he did not give up his assumption regarding the coming of a kingdom at the divinely appointed hour (cf. Matthew 24:36). Where the immortal soul would stay between physical expiration and that great day is not divulged. Jesus' followers evidently assumed it would be in Sheol, where in their thinking all the dead abode. It was much later that the idea that the righteous dead were somehow populating ethereal heavens came into vogue (cf. Revelation 6:9–11). The first corollary attitude of Jesus in connection with life beyond death was that there was immortality for the inward man though the flesh die, decay and disappear.

b) JESUS EXPECTED HIS OWN DEATH AND RESURRECTION.—A second attitude which stemmed from this principle regarded his own death. Need we be branded heretic for assuming that his thoughts in regard to his own death and resurrection reveal his attitude toward the same experience for each individual? Of course, a supernaturalist Christian will rebel at this suggestion, for his faith is predicated upon the assumption that Jesus is deity and that therefore what appears mysterious and inconceivable for the individual must be due to Jesus' deity. But it is the conviction of this writer that we need to be bold and take Jesus as we find him, and not let human theology confuse the issue.

Gospel records reveal a psychologically probable life-situation for Jesus. In the midst of the fast-moving events of the confession of Peter (cf. Mark 8:27–30 and parallels) and the Transfiguration (cf. Mark 9:2–13 and parallels), Jesus shared his premonitions of his death (cf. Mark 8:31–33 and parallels). In the light of all the evidence Jesus saw that death was practically inevitable. The records appear to indicate Jesus' increasing precautionary measures, especially during the so-called last week, so that his death would not take place until he was ready and spiritually prepared for the ordeal. He had to prepare his intimate disciples for this situation, since he was relatively very young. Death in his thirties would come as a shock to them. He must prepare them, now that he was certain. It is in this certainty of death that his own attitude toward death shows up.

Now we must seek to state his attitude regarding his "resurrection." This was certainly an attitude of faith, and a faith built on an attitude that there was life after death. It would appear also that Jesus did not conceive that his life after death was to await any resuscitation of the body—despite the age-long Christian discussion of his resurrection-body and the possibility of the flesh going to heaven. He appears to consider his life after physical death to be spiritual in nature. And to this day, Christianity survives upon the reality of the Christian's certainty of fellowship and personal communication with a spiritual Christ, unseen by physical eyes yet consciously felt by the human spirit still encased in a body. Jesus likewise appears to regard this ongoing aspect of his person to be that which had been enclosed in his body, which died on the cross. In other words, his spiritual nature or his being is immortal, untainted by the moment of physical death, and is indestructible.

c) ETERNAL IDENTITY.—Thus we see that Jesus assumed that there was an immortal portion of the human being which did not die with the flesh but could be counted upon to survive and continue its existence in very much its same basic character. Thus we must believe that Jesus assumed the retention of the identities of the person beyond physical death. Yet the physical aspects, such as sex (cf. Mark 12:25 and parallels), were halted or eradicated at death. Persons would continue to have fellowship, respect and love for each other without regard for age, sex, status or race. Presumably they would all have contact and fellowship with God face to face. The spiritual community and communion of the life beyond will ultimately be the experience and reality of the physically living as it is presumably existent now "in heavenly places." This is why Jesus expected to rejoin his followers at some future date to share in the Kingdom of God on earth. This is why the Jew still thinks in very material terms regarding the Kingdom of God. For the Jew, the Kingdom of God does not exist unless it is incarnate in "Israel" and the daily life of "the chosen people." This is why the Roman Catholic Church maintains the dogma that apart from "the Church" there is no "Kingdom" and membership in the Church indicates citizenship in that divine Kingdom. Protestantism, however, reflects Jesus' position more faithfully. The Kingdom of God is primarily spiritual in nature. It may exist on earth; it exists already in God's presence; it will find ultimate expression on earth when God's destiny comes to fruition, but it really does not depend upon its physical manifestations for existence. The day when it will be the actual Kingdom of mankind on earth has not yet arrived.

Spiritually, individuals can enter it now. Human attempts to manifest its presence in their personal lives and their communal groups can be undertaken, but they are all poor copies of the divine reality of the Kingdom of God.

Jesus' faith was predicated therefore on the principle that there is life after death, and that being is immortal. He assumed that in his expectation regarding his own future life and that of all human beings and the present-future kingdom of God in its interpersonal relationships.

A Concluding Remark

Before we conclude this chapter, a warning is pertinent. We have deliberately placed this warning at the end in order for the reader to secure a positive statement of the matter regarding basic principles and attitudes before such a presentation is confronted with a definite challenge.

The challenge of the problem is this. It still has to be proved that the attitudes of Jesus which lead and point back to the fundamental principles presented here are the *only* fruits of those principles. What we are faced with is this: In Jesus' teachings we can gather and establish certain recognizable basic attitudes which Jesus invariably expressed. Our task, then, was to attempt to state what appear to be the established principles upon which these various attitudes depend. This seemed practical and possible; but once these basic principles had been determined and identified there was no reasonable certainty that the attitudes which emanated from them in Jesus' life would be the same for any other individual. Somewhere between the principles and the desired attitudes there is many a deflection. Just how to prevent these deflections is still a secret of the universe. If there was assurance that certain attitudes and actions would naturally express certain guiding principles in life, we could seek to establish these standard principles in life, then in the souls of men, and expect as the normal result innumerable Christ-like individuals and a human society of righteousness and peace worthy of being called the Kingdom of God on earth.

The challenge must not thwart the sincere Christian, however. The principles and attitudes which form the foundations upon which Jesus' faith took expression in word and deed must ever be the humble yearning of the penitent heart of the young Christian.

EPILOGUE

A very striking and pertinent painting characterizes the message of this book; it is entitled "The Lost Sheep" and is the work of Alfred Soord. The viewer senses that he stands securely above the central figure in the scene, looking down a rather precipitous mountainside into the valley far below. One's attention is drawn to the squatted figure of a local shepherd with his back to the onlooker. The painter skillfully leads our eyes down the right arm to a loving, sensitive hand which grasps toward a frightened and helpless lamb caught in a thicket. Overhead in the upper center of the picture hovers a hungry vulture waiting to pounce upon the defenseless animal. All this brings to mind Jesus' parable of the Good Shepherd who leaves ninety-nine secure sheep in his flock and endangers his life to rescue the one that has gone astray (Luke 15:3–7, Matthew 18:10–14).

There the average observer halts his interpretation of the painting, for a familiar message appears clear and definitive. Yet the artist has consciously or unconsciously portrayed a great truth in simply filling in the factual aspect of the situation. The shepherd looks anxiously at the ensnared lamb. In order to keep his balance as he lowers himself cautiously toward the thicket, the shepherd tightens his grasp to the security of a protruding rock. The muscles in that arm are taut as he reaches down. Upon the security of the rock depends the safety of the shepherd, as well as of the lamb. More boldly stated, that which saved the lamb was not merely the shepherd's concern for the lamb but the wise action and the strong reliance of the shepherd upon the rock. In reality it was the Shepherd's *faith* that saved not only the shepherd but the lamb as well. That is the message of this book.

In Jesus of Nazareth is the hope of the individual and society of every age. Mankind has been enlightened and inspired through his life, thought and ministry. The writer of the fourth

Gospel may not have been recording the actual words of the historic Jesus, but he was stating a fact nevertheless when he had Jesus say, "I am the way, and the truth, and the life" (John 14:6). By the quality of his *life,* men have sought his secret for living. His thought has helped men to see the *truth* of God more clearly; man has been able to grasp something of the truth and wisdom which make life meaningful and refreshing. With new perspectives and revelations man has gained intellectual stature worthy of his sonship to God. Certainly Jesus can speak with authority as to the *way* such wisdom and righteousness can be gained. His own life of faith had been tried and tested. The success of his way of life assured him that it was *the* way of God, and he vigorously sought to share it. In his own words, he said, "Take my yoke upon you, and learn from me" (Matthew 11:29, cf. John 13:15). Only as we learn from Jesus how to live by faith will we truly lay hold of that power that transforms our present existence into meaningful living in accordance with the divine purpose. Then comes into existence a Kingdom under God made up of individuals who are truly sons of God. These sons will reflect the Father to a degree approximating Jesus, for the same faith-living will bear similar fruit. As we see God in Jesus, so will the unbelievers of mankind see in all Christians the marks of the image of God.

The acquisition of such a faith and its resultant conduct is no easy matter. Mimicking will avail nothing. It is superficial to proclaim: "Believe in the Lord Jesus, and you will be saved" (Acts 16:31). Intellectual affirmations do not engender such life-changing faith. There are many who believe *on* him; these give intellectual affirmation as to the identity and nature of the Christ in Jesus, but acceptance of facts does not change people's lives. There are many who believe *in* him. They are ready to affirm the facts which Jesus stated, which Jesus lived. But for most of these people this is a simple affirmation of an ideal. For them Jesus was different; certainly he was different from them. Therefore, what he said was true for him, but they are sinners, living in a different century under different circumstances. Or again, they believe what Jesus said, for they were the ideals toward which men struggled; but the ideals seem too impractical in this present age. What he said is true enough, they agree, but they feel forced to compromise for the present. Jesus, however, was no idealist; what he said was true—not because *he* said it but because it is inherently true. Nothing Jesus taught or advocated was impractical or idealistic, for *he* had tested it in his own daily living. In frank terms: he was not revealing a set of abstract truths, straight from some supernatural place; rather, he was sharing a faith whose truth was revealed because it was truth inherent in the universe. Only when we personally seek to believe *with* Jesus will we be exposed to such empowering faith that our lives will naturally and normally begin to express a life like his in the divinely intended nature of an image of God.

It is at this very point that what this author likes to think of as "the art of attunement" comes into full significance. Put into the very words of Jesus, the idea is this: "Truly, I say to you, unless you turn and become like children, you will never enter the kingdom of heaven" (Matthew 18:3, cf. Mark 10:15, Luke 18:17). This attuning process is the dire need of the present day, when bewildered humanity seeks security and peace of mind as poor substitutes for the atonement of God. Such attunement, moreover, is no simple or single matter either. To "turn and become like children" (Matthew 18:3) is no simple act. Such humility, such eagerness, such naïveté and such alertness children do have! They consciously and unconsciously mimic and relive the attitudes and actions of their ideals. So Jesus lived, as a child of God. So Jesus sought to share with mankind that we might act as true children of God through the art of attunement.

This art of attunement has three steps which, however, must be sought simultaneously. There is the need for an attuning of the *heart*, the *mind* and the *will* to their divine counterparts. Attunement of the *heart* is the acquiring of a quality of character like unto God's spirit, both in the individual personality and in his interpersonal relationships. In actuality, it is the sincere acquisition of a divine type of love. One of the marks of this attunement is a native respect for personality as such. As the Apostle Paul wrote: "There is neither Jew nor Greek, there is neither slave nor free, there is neither male nor female; for you are all one in Christ Jesus" (Galatians 3:28). This is simple to state and intellectually to affirm, but very difficult to live. In the same spirit Jesus spoke of loving one's enemies (cf. Matthew 5:44–45, Luke 6:27–28,35), of turning the other cheek (cf. Matthew 5:39, Luke 6:29), of going the second mile (cf. Matthew 5:41), of forgiving seventy times seven times (cf. Matthew 18:22). Living in this spirit brings the art of attunement of the heart into full focus. It is no easy matter. It is not achieved by stiff self-discipline, but only through intimate spiritual fellowship with God. By means of this so-called attunement process one ultimately gains a naturalness in this way of life. Jesus tried it. It worked. He endeavored to share it. It became his good news, his gospel. He was so successful in his own daily living of it that his disciples through the years have not been able to make the distinction between the nature of God and the nature of Jesus. In Jesus' manifestation of divine love, we see the nature of God's love.

Then there is the attunement of the *mind*. Reading the words of Jesus as recorded in the Gospels, one becomes aware of a marked gulf between Jesus' attitudes and perspectives and one's own. When you read that Jesus said, "Be not anxious for the morrow" (cf. Luke 12:22, Matthew 6:25), are you? Can you? When Jesus sees deep significance in a little child, do you? Can you? When Jesus talks of doing good to those who spitefully use you, can you? Do you? Is Jesus' attitude toward possessions yours? Do you respond to wickedness with the same combination of judgment and mercy that characterizes Jesus' response? Check your own attitudes and perspectives with those of Jesus. Do you normally and naturally "believe *with* him"? If not, then attunement is greatly needed. The Apostle Paul put it this way: "Let this mind be in you, which was also in Christ Jesus" (Philippians 2:5, A.V.). And again, "Do not be conformed to this world but be transformed by the renewal of your mind, that you may prove what is the will of God, what is good and acceptable and perfect" (Romans 12:2).

The most difficult aspect of this attunement process, however, is that of the *will*. Mankind seems to be able with some effort to gain some of God's spirit, and to hold in high esteem the ideas and attitudes of God and Jesus, but to will the Will of God— man never quite masters that. Yet it is at this very point, in addition to the attunements of the affections and the intellect, that the life-changing power releases that potentiality inherent in the individual which makes him an image of the Heavenly Father. It was this release that marked the early Christians (cf. Acts 4:31). The new life-potential which was unleashed when men willed the Will of God became so wondrously fresh and inspiring that even Paul could not believe he was the same person. "It is no longer I that live, but Christ liveth in me" (Galatians 2:20, A.S.V.). Jesus' recorded prayers in Gethsemane (cf. Mark 14:36, Matthew 26:39,42, Luke 22:42) and on the cross (cf. Luke 23:46) indicate that this attunement of the will was no easy art. Even he in his hour of trial needed to attune more delicately his will to that of his Heavenly Father. Selfishness and self-will so easily hinder realization of the fullest potentials of our being.

We can see clearly that this art of attunement is a lifetime process. It is the actual nature of faith as Jesus experienced it and sought to make it known to mankind. The faith of Jesus is the art of maturation through the interplay of persons, man and his God. Jesus would have us learn from him this art of attunement, which is a process of steady growth and refinement by an earnest person who finds the significance and truth of the faith of Jesus.

Jesus said:

> Why do you call me "Lord, Lord," and not do what I tell you? Every one who comes to me and hears my words and does them, I will show you what he is like: he is like a man building a house, who dug deep, and laid the foundation upon rock; and when a flood arose, the stream broke against

that house, and could not shake it, because it had been well built. But he who hears and does not do them is like a man who built a house on the ground without a foundation; against which the stream broke, and immediately it fell, and the ruin of that house was great. (Luke 6:46–49)

Again he said: "No one who puts his hand to the plow and looks back is fit for the kingdom of God" (Luke 9:62). Therefore—

... blessed are your eyes, for they see, and your ears, for they hear. Truly, I say to you, many prophets and righteous men longed to see what you see, and did not see it, and to hear what you hear, and did not hear it. (Matthew 13:16-17)

Let the faith of Jesus be yours!